309

THE URGE TO PERSECUTE

Books by A. Powell Davies

AMERICAN DESTINY
THE FAITH OF AN UNREPENTANT LIBERAL
AMERICA'S REAL RELIGION
THE URGE TO PERSECUTE

published by The Beacon Press

MAN'S VAST FUTURE
THE TEMPTATION TO BE GOOD

published by Farrar, Straus & Young

The Urge to Persecute

by

A. Powell Davies

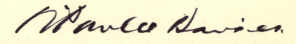

THE BEACON PRESS   **BOSTON**

Contents

Preface

A minister of religion has many duties, some of which are quiet and inconspicuous, and no one minds if he is zealous in attending to them. If, however, he performs with equal zeal the duty of applying religion to a public issue and is widely heard, he will be sharply criticized. This he expects — not because he thinks that he has overstepped the boundaries of his ministerial obligations but because he knows that religion, if it be authentic, is greatly feared and widely misconstrued.

The reason for this is not obscure. Religion measures all things by its claim for righteousness. Since such a claim, to many folks, seems too exacting, they try to set a limit to it. Religion must be walled in, preferably beneath the roofs of churches. The Kingdom of God must be a prayer, not a program; justice must be an aspiration, not an intention; and love must be a mood and not on any account a motivation. If, therefore, a minister applies his religion to the factors which are shaping history, rebuking unrighteousness where it is most damaging, he is told that this is not his province.

The answer is, in the first place, that such an argument does not make sense and whatever does not make sense is bad religion. How could it make sense that a minister should plead for righteousness in his own parish and keep his silence when righteousness is being mocked in the total sum of all the parishes that constitute a nation? Moreover, no minister is confined within the boundaries of a single parish. He vows himself to serve the brotherhood of man. Wherever, then, the brotherhood of man requires his service, he must try to serve it.

There are those who say that this may be, but still the duty of a minister is to " stay out of politics " and " preach his sermons from the Bible." Without conceding this, I feel bound to point out that those who demand it have very little knowledge of the Bible. What do they think of the preacher, Nathan, who went to King David, and pointing the finger at him, said, " Thou art the man "? What do they say of Elijah, who publicly condemned Queen Jezebel? Or of Amos, a preacher self-ordained, who went to the capital city of Samaria to tell the nation's rulers that God had grown weary of their sins? Or of Isaiah, a preacher from an aristocratic family who was nevertheless a reformer and who told King Hezekiah that religion had a place in foreign policy? Or of Jeremiah who foretold the doom of a nation that forsook its moral principles? Or — to come to a conclusive instance — of Jesus who not only *talked* about cleansing the Temple but who took " a whip of cords " and drove the grafters from its precincts in complete defiance of the alliance of priests and politicians?

Any minister worthy of his ordination will take these as his examples, and knowing the Bible better than his critics, will pray for the wisdom and courage to be as forthright and as faithful as the Bible preachers. Even, however, if the Bible tradition were otherwise, and if there had never been any John Knoxes, Savonarolas, or Theodore Parkers, the condition of the modern world requires that preachers deal with public questions. We live at a time of indescribable peril and with almost no margin for error. Even at best, we may not avoid calamities. We do not know. But we do know — or should — that only through calm, deliberate wisdom, inspired by a benevolent justice and an unflagging zeal for righteousness can we hope to be saved. That, above all, is why religion, even though its spokesmen are fallible and make no other claim than that they speak what conscience has commanded, must be extended to the uttermost. Less than that would be betrayal.

We know — and some of us have long since known — that Communism is the enemy. We know, too, that the enemy is resourceful as well as evil. We know that we are being conspired against. Some of us have seen — myself included — how dangerous is this enemy since the time of its emergence. In my own case, because I was fortunately guided, I learned to recognize the evil of Communism at the time of the Russian Revolution. Later, in London between school and college, I had exceptional privileges. I heard the issues of these new and revolutionary trends debated. I believed that no good would come of Communism, and I have never faltered in so thinking. My reasons are — and always were — moral and spiritual. Economic questions I regard as important only as they affect the moral and spiritual. As it seemed to me, and still does, the Russian Revolution was really a counter-revolution — the one true revolution of the modern age being the American Revolution, which founded a society upon the rights and liberties of individual men.

Since these rights are moral rights, to transgress them is not only repugnant to our political principles but, from the standpoint of religion, grievously unrighteous, or to use the old word, sinful. The current persecutions, therefore, have inevitably struck sharply at the consciences of preachers, and some of them have spoken out.

As one such, I have felt prompted, this summer, to try to understand the persecutions in the wider context — historical, psychological and moral — of the total crisis of the modern age. This book is the outcome.

I am under obligation to many friends for their suggestions and encouragement, and to antagonists and critics for their useful stimulation. Audiences throughout the country have helped me, by their questions, to focus the issues more sharply, and their generous reception of what I had to say has fortified my belief that there are multitudes of Americans who will never bow down the knee to tyranny.

I am deeply indebted to Miss Jane Grey Wheeler, my Assistant at All Souls' Church, for untiring co-operation in the preparation of the manuscript and for sharing the research; and to Mrs. Stuart Haydon and Miss Vesta Magnusson for looking up references and for assistance to Miss Wheeler in preparing the index and reading proof.

To my congregation in Washington, unfailing in encouragement and inspiration, my gratitude can never be enough.

A. POWELL DAVIES

Washington, D. C.
October 15, 1953

THE URGE TO PERSECUTE

Introduction: The Climate of Fear

Communism: Reality and Pretext

The possibility that the people of the United States might be converted to Communism is too remote for serious consideration. Only a small minority has ever been attracted to it. The real danger is from abroad. There, in his stronghold, the Communist enemy, resolved upon world dominion, is becoming equipped with weapons of annihilation. No reason exists for believing that if it serves his ends he will hesitate to use them. This is the threat upon which we should be concentrating.

The fact is, however, that the attention of the American people, far from being absorbed by this major threat of Communist aggression, has been directed to the relatively minor one of Communism in America. Congressional committees, instead of inquiring into the truly frightening deficiencies in our national security which make us mortally vulnerable to the attack of the Communist from abroad, are conducting investigations upon the preposterous basis that the real enemy is the Communist at home. This could scarcely be excused even if its effect were mere irrelevance: the urgency of the genuine peril is too great. But the fact is that the investigations have seriously harmed us.

At a moment when the Communist danger from abroad requires not only strenuous military preparations but our utmost efforts in diplomacy, the irresponsible activities of one of these committees has undermined our diplomatic service. At a time when the confidence of our European allies is essential to us, the behavior of emissaries of this same committee has unsettled it. When the President appointed the ablest and most experienced man available to our embassy in Moscow, the chairman of this committee attempted to frustrate it.

This last instance, of course, is only one out of many, and its distinction is that the attempted obstruction was a failure. The campaign of hindrance and intimidation has on the whole succeeded: so much so that the State Department and the Foreign Service, upon which we must rely in our diplomatic struggle with the Communists abroad, have been severely damaged. If what has been done were clearly perceived, the question it would raise is how so much harm could be done without deliberate intent. Certainly, the damage could not have been worse if it had been contrived by Communists. The presumption, however, at least by present definitions, is that it was not treason.

Nevertheless, if calamity befalls and we survive it, it may very well be that the American people — or those that remain — will demand a reckoning with the men who robbed them of their strength and broke their unity and undermined them. Treason may then be given a wider definition.

Meanwhile, what is the truth about Communism in America? According to the men who pretend that it is our greatest danger, Communism has infiltrated our entire national life. This is perverse and fantastic. Even if they were free to do their worst, there are not enough Communists.[1]

---

[1] According to the FBI, the Communist Party in the United States had 31,608 members in 1951.

It is true that, for a small group, Communists in the United States did for a while score some remarkable achievements. They entrenched themselves in certain of the labor unions; they had influence in literature and the arts; they penetrated some of the professions; they formed — or captured — the " front " organizations and beguiled Americans of all shades of opinion into joining them; they carried on some deadly espionage; and a few of them worked their way into the government.

But most of this — indeed, almost all — is in the past. Communism in the United States is decisively discredited. As Mr. George Kennan, a foremost expert on Communism, has put it, " for the Western world . . . the Soviet threat today is almost exclusively a physical one, a military-territorial one along traditional patterns, *not one of the power of ideas.*" [2] Except for spies and saboteurs — who are the concern, not of Congressional committees, which are not equipped to deal with them, but of the FBI and the Department of Justice — Communism in America is of minor importance.

Minor, that is, except in one particular: it provides the pretext for those who exploit fear and whose real aim is to destroy traditional American liberalism — the same liberalism which, until recently, the Communists were trying to manipulate to serve their ends. The former success of Communists in deceiving liberals — not all liberals, but a sizable number — is made the basis for identifying the two; although in fact they are worlds apart, guilt is imputed through former association.

Seldom do the Congressional committees unmask an

[2] Address to conference on Soviet imperialism at School of Advanced International Studies of the Johns Hopkins University, August 10, 1953. (Italics added.)

actual Communist. They maintain their anti-Communist coloration by haling before them, from time to time, what might be called warmed-over ex-Communists, through whose testimony they hope to implicate people who have not at any time been Communists but whose views they do not like. Sheltered by Congressional immunity, they make charges without foundation and insinuations that are slanderous.

Instead of being guided by the purpose for which Congressional committees were constituted — that of gathering information necessary and useful in the making of laws — they sit as extra-judicial tribunals and examine witnesses without being obliged to respect the traditional provisions which our fathers, in their wisdom and out of long experience, prescribed as necessary safeguards in our courts.

As a result of their activities, the committees have produced, especially in the government service, crippling tensions and anxieties; suspicion and mistrust are everywhere; they have created a climate of fear. If the Communists, in providing the pretext for the investigations, intended this result, it must be counted their most notable accomplishment. Nothing they achieved in the heyday of their " popular fronts " can compare with it as service to the Communist cause.

Political Comprehension and Moral Realism

The committees, however, are not alone to blame.[3] They could not have done what they have if the American

---

[3] In using the inevitable term "committees," I do not mean that all committee members are equally culpable. Representative Doyle, for instance, was obviously opposed to the procedure of the Un-American Activities Committee in Bishop Oxnam's hearing. Members of the Sub-Committee of which Senator McCarthy is chairman have walked out of

people — or a sufficient number of them — had not permitted and encouraged it. They could not have done it without the confusion — earlier — and timidity — later — of many liberals. And the chief guilt, of course, lies with the Communists.

But it is also true that the phenomenon of persecution has arisen in a set of circumstances which particularly invited it. From a historical viewpoint, it is a part of the complex of responses to a situation of crisis. Psychologically, it is a release of hostile impulses as a response to unwanted conditions. Morally, it is a transference of guilt to justify the rejection of difficult ethical requirements. Spiritually, it is an expression of emptiness.

It is the aim of this book, therefore, to view the current persecutions in their wider context and to identify the factors, external and internal, historical and psychological, which have had a share in causing them. It is not intended, and for the purpose in hand is not required, that the story of the persecutions be recounted. Only occasionally and as an illustration will an individual case be introduced. Other writers are taking up the sequential narrative and the personal portrayals.

My own aim is both broader and simpler. It arises from my situation. As a preacher, I have spoken out against the persecutions and have been a part of the continuing controversy; as a person resident in Washington and with a wide acquaintance, I have known the facts and understood what lay behind them; as a parish minister whose liberal views have never been concealed from the com-

---

it in disgust. But the reader will know from his newspaper what the current situation is in these respects: and he will understand that by "committees" I mean these entities in what has been their typical behavior.

munity, I have been frequently sought out by those in need of sympathy and counsel; as one who has looked often and for many years into the inner realities of human lives, I know that there is nothing important in this world that is not traceable at last to the conflict of good and evil in individual men and women.

Of nothing is this more true than of the urge to persecute.   Hence what I say, although presented in the context of history, including the history I have seen in the making, is based upon the profound conviction that the crisis of our time is moral and spiritual.   Only when political comprehension is imbued with moral realism do we see the true nature of events and what they require of us. The standpoint of this analysis, therefore, is that of moral realism.

The Headlines and the People

But to a considerable number of Americans, carried away by the current " anti-Communist " sensationalism, neither morality nor realism have recently been meaningful.   The newspapers scream out the charges.   Two hundred and five, or eighty-one, or fifty-seven card-carrying Communists in the State Department.   An honored general " a front man for traitors " and " a living lie."   A widely known bishop serves God on Sundays and the Communist cause the rest of the week.   American diplomatists abroad are betraying their country.   Communist plots in schools and colleges.   Washington a hot-bed of subversive activities.

But then, it is urged, these charges — even if they *are* sensational — do they not help in " rooting out Reds "? Isn't it a good thing to " wake up Washington " and make life harder for some of these people who are " soft on Com-

munists "? Don't government workers need " shaking up "
and doesn't the government require " cleaning out "?
What you see in the headlines may be a bit extreme — but
it gets things done, doesn't it? Who would have " got
after " the Communists if these extremists had not started
it?

The fact that the FBI has long since been alert to
Communist infiltration is not remembered; the thoroughness — even the rigor — of the loyalty and security investigations is overlooked; the report of Representative Bartel
Jonkman (Republican, Michigan), of the House Foreign
Affairs Committee, to the Eightieth Congress (1948) that
the State Department was clear of " subversives, Communists, fellow-travellers, sympathizers, and persons whose
services are not for the best interests of the United States " [4]
has been little noticed.

Nor is it reflected upon much that the assertions in the
headlines are not true. If they serve a purpose, does it
matter whether they are true? It is forgotten that a purpose served by lies must be an evil purpose. Americans
dazed by the headlines do not see that each new falsehood
is a blow at national security and an attack upon their own
free institutions. They do not see that the assault upon
departments of their government is not a " shaking-up " or
" cleaning-out " of " elements " but something that is happening to *people*. They do not realize that the people to
whom it is happening are not " subversives " but loyal
citizens: the citizens to whom, in many cases, the rest of
us must look in out-thinking, out-planning and out-per-
forming the enemy in a time of mortal danger. They do
not understand that if the courage and confidence of these

[4] *Congressional Record*, Aug. 2, 1948, p. 9643.

people is turned into timidity and anxiety, their minds will be fettered and their initiative crippled precisely when this is most damaging.

When Everybody Is Wondering about Everybody

It is difficult to see the realities when you are blinded by the headlines. But it is impossible to mistake them when you meet them in the lives of *people*. For my own part, the effect of these headlines and of what lies behind them was most emphatically conveyed not by the more tragic of the cases that came to my attention, but by a man who, upon entering my office, greeted me with the words, " No problem! Just came to say goodbye." He was leaving the government service, not because he was being investigated or had run into any kind of difficulty, but because he had " figured that it made no sense waiting around here until something began to happen to you."

" What might happen? " I asked. " I have no idea," he replied, " any more than a good many other people who suddenly found themselves in trouble."

" Well," I observed, hoping that there would be no harm in a little banter, " if it were not for the way things are in this city, nowadays, I would be inclined to quote to you from the Book of Proverbs. You probably know the saying anyway. ' The wicked flee when no man pursueth.' Maybe that's what they thought when you handed in your resignation. They probably noted it at the end of your record! "

" No," he said, with a rather wry smile. " I'm not running away from anything. Though as a matter of fact, I wouldn't blame you if you wondered about it quite seriously. We've reached the stage where everybody is wondering about everybody, and it wouldn't be strange if you were, too. You don't particularly know me. I've been attending your church but I'm not a member. I don't even know that you recognized me when I came in here this afternoon."

I said nothing. It was true that I had not actually recognized him. I thought I had seen him before but could not have sworn to it.

"Anyway," he continued, " I've never had a pro-Communist thought in my life. And I've never joined any of the ' fronts.' That isn't because I was cleverer than other people but because I'm not a ' joiner.' It's true that I think there's plenty gone wrong with this country lately, but you can think that and still be an American. My loyalty is O.K. So is my ' security.' In fact, I'm rather a conventional sort of ' character,' I guess — at least by modern standards — and so far as I know, I've done nothing worth hiding! But I do happen to be placed where I might make a decision that some one on a ' Committee ' wouldn't like. I don't know what it would be — but neither did some other people until they suddenly found out. I don't want that kind of trouble. When you get into it, you don't ever get out. You are used for whatever purpose the ' Committee ' people have in mind. You can be brought back again and again. You can have your testimony twisted to make it bad for your friends. Twisted questions get into the papers; simple answers don't — and sometimes, there isn't any simple answer: they fix it that way. I've seen what happened to the others. So I've been quietly looking for a job — while the going was good — and I've got one in — " [5]

[5] Name of locality withheld. In this narrative, as in those that follow, all facts that might lead to identification have been omitted or disguised. This is necessary to protect those who have come to me in confidence. But no changes have been made, either in fact or emphasis, which affect the substance or the impression conveyed to the reader.

I asked him how he felt about leaving the government service. He told me what I had supposed he would: that he had expected to make it his lifelong career. But he was no longer doing his work properly; it was impossible. "What you try to do," he said, "is keep away from everything that is not routine. Even in routine, you do nothing that leaves you responsible; you see to it that the responsibility is always with somebody else. Maybe *he* doesn't want to be responsible either. So nobody is responsible and what you get is a certain amount of activity, enough to keep busy, but you are not really doing anything. And you get tired — or at least I did — of being everlastingly afraid."

"Who will take your place?" I asked. "Will he feel differently?"

My visitor looked at me for a moment. "I know what you mean," he said. "Somebody has to stay and fight it out and you think it should have been me. You may be right. It's possible that that's partly why I came to see you — to make my confession! But I'm not a quitter, really. It hasn't been easy. I have a family and I'm getting no younger. I know a man who tried for a year to get a job after he left the government. He is working now at [naming some manual work]. I don't think he can stand it very long."

I told him that I was not passing judgment upon him. I just wanted to know how he felt about that side of the question. And I wondered how many other people were trying to find positions outside the government.

"Well," he said, "a lot of them just can't. The job they're doing is the one job they know. But they wish they were nearer to retirement! Of course, the State Department is where it is worst. That's where they are *really* scared. They hope that if they keep very, very quiet, they won't be noticed."

"Yes," I rejoined, "and that's where it's doing us the most damage. Frightened people win no victories — diplomatic or any other."

"No," said my visitor. "Perhaps our best hope is that the Communists scare each other even more than we do."

After he had left, I reflected sadly that this was indeed the most hopeful factor in our situation. Communism could be self-defeating. But so could we. It was not much of a hope. If it were true, as this man's visit seemed to indicate, that people who were not in trouble of any kind and had nothing to hide were either leaving the government or wished they could, then demoralization had already gone much farther than I had realized.

I have given the reader a rather full report of this interview because it is uncomplicated by any imputation of disloyalty — or, I might add, by any question of inefficiency, for my visitor had been a capable and valued public servant. Yet the reader can multiply it many times and I am confident that he will not be exaggerating what is happening in the government service.

The Pressure for Conformity

The need for a screening process, in the case at any rate of those who occupy so-called "sensitive" positions, is, of course, obvious. But it could have been far more intelligent and, except in cases where there was something to hide, much less intimidating. As a recent report on the loyalty-security program has put it:

"If the tensions of the time demand some temporary

sacrifice of basic freedoms, let us never forget that their maintenance is as necessary to national security in a free democratic society as is the protection of our physical safety; let us never accept the sacrifice with complacence." [6]

To all too great an extent, however, the sacrifice *has* been accepted with complacence — and the sacrifice has been too large. Increasingly, loyalty has come to be confused with conformity and even with mediocrity. Evidence of independent judgment, while not a conclusive sign of guilt, has become an indication that more rigorous investigation may be necessary. An adventurous mind, unless it can conceal its animation, invites suspicion. Self-confidence can be a handicap.

I think, for instance, of a lady working at a routine job in a government agency which had nothing to do with national security. She had overcome a severe physical handicap and had taught herself to do her rather tedious work efficiently. In due time, on the usual basis, she was investigated.

It was discovered that many years before, when she had been more prosperous and was resident abroad, she and her husband, since deceased, had entertained some radical politicians in their home, some of whom may have had a friendly interest in the Soviet Union. Upon being questioned, the lady not only admitted that the charge was correct but insisted that, as a free American, she had a perfect right to entertain whom she would. Furthermore, she enjoyed listening to conflicts of opinion, and, although

---

[6] Eleanor Bontecou, *The Federal Loyalty-Security Program* (N.Y.: Cornell University Press, 1953). (One of a series of eight volumes, prepared under a Rockefeller grant, reporting " the impact upon our civil liberties of current governmental programs designed to insure internal security and to explore and control disloyal or subversive conduct.")

truth was a hard thing to come by and you never quite knew when you had arrived at it, discussion might sometimes disclose a little of it.

Her examiners wanted to know what she thought about Russia. She said that she had never been there and had no basis for an opinion. What, then, did she gather from the usual sources of information, newspapers, radio, and the like? She answered that she did not place reliance in any of these media of communication; they were often wrong. She did not know which stories to believe and which to disbelieve.

Obviously, she was a difficult lady to interrogate. A lifetime of independence had formed her character in the classical American mold, and she was afraid of nobody. She simply said exactly what she thought and saw no reason for doing otherwise. In any case, it was perfectly evident — except to her dull investigators — that she was incapable of conspiracy. After all, a conspirator, to be useful, must sometimes be able to hold her tongue. Moreover, her work afforded her no opportunity whatever for conspiracy. It was entirely non-secret and completely routine.

Nevertheless, she was dismissed. Yet all that she was guilty of was the exercise of freedom — classical American freedom! She had refused to conform to the new timidities.

She was later re-instated. Whether this was as a result of protests made or would have occurred in their absence when the matter came up for review, I have no way of knowing; but I think that an injustice as obvious as this would have been remedied. The people engaged in loyalty-security investigations must not be placed under a blanket indictment; many of them were conscientious and enlightened citizens and their work was often difficult. It is to be hoped that the new arrangement, recently introduced, will be an improvement — though under the conditions at present prevailing, it is hard to see how it can. But however that may be, the point to be made is that an atmosphere exists — and is growing worse — in which a government servant, if he does not want his loyalty suspected, finds it prudent to take refuge in a colorless conformity.

There are, however, pressures towards conformity of an uglier sort. Here, we can give examples from the public record — which I could match with similar ones confided to me in private interviews. The questions are those of loyalty investigators quoted in a dissenting opinion of Judge Henry W. Edgerton of the United States Court of Appeals for the District of Columbia: [7]

" Do you read a good many books? " " What books do you read? " " What newspapers do you buy or subscribe to? " " Do you think that Russian Communism is likely to succeed? " " How do you explain the fact that you have an album of Paul Robeson records in your home? " " Is it not true that you lived next door to and therefore were closely associated with a member of the I.W.W.? "

From the same source may be cited the fact that a woman employee of the government was under suspicion of disloyalty because, at the time of the siege of Stalingrad, she collected money for Russian war relief while at the same time she was collecting money for British and French relief. Another employee was taken to task because he was a member of Consumers' Union and did not believe in

---

[7] *Bailey v. Richardson et al.*, 86 U.S. App. D.C. 248, 268; 183 F. 2d 46.

racial discrimination. Still another employee — who did lose her job and who lost her appeal two-to-one — was asked with considerable insistence what her views were about the segregation of blood in blood banks.

Evidently, a government worker, to feel really safe in his job, should not only conform to the most orthodox of opinions but should also adopt the most reactionary of prejudices.

How to Prove Your Patriotism

If, beyond conforming, which after all is rather negative, a government worker wishes to give evidence of positive zeal in the service of this new and morbid brand of patriotism, provision has been made for it.

In a report released by the Un-American Activities Committee, in the fall of 1952, it is disclosed that ten employees of the Signal Corps Intelligence Agency signed a petition to Congress requesting investigation of that Agency and " corrective measures to remove all subversive elements and security risks therefrom."

Specifically, seven civilian employees of the Agency were accused. And so the investigation was begun — as indeed it should have been if there were genuine and substantial questions. But when the investigation was complete — an investigation which the Committee called " intensive " — nothing was found against the accused employees except the unproved charges of their fellow-workers.

One might suppose that the Committee would have been very happy at this outcome: the less disloyalty there is, the more a patriotic American should rejoice; and one would expect that the Committee would be rather disdainful of the ten employees who made the accusations. But no! The

Committee warmly commends them and says that they are worthy of " emulation by all in Government employ." This means, if it means anything, that whoever has a baseless charge that he might make against a fellow-worker is encouraged to make it. Every government worker should therefore prove his patriotism by expressing his mistrust of seven, at least, among his fellow-workers.

How interesting this report must have been to officials of the Soviet Embassy if they chanced to read of it in their morning newspapers! Except, of course, that they could not enjoy it without uneasiness. After all, how could they know? Someone might have been accusing *them* right at that moment, somewhere in Moscow, because " that's the way it's done in Russia." In Russia? " Yes," says the government employee, reading the same newspaper as he rides to work on the bus through the broad avenues of Washington, " that's the way it's done in Russia." And he wonders which seven of his fellow-workers it would be least wicked to accuse.

Unhappily, there are Americans who applaud this reckless kind of accusation and who think it *is* evidence of patriotism. Actually, the secret motive — sometimes hidden even from themselves — that prompts their applause is a vicarious kind of " bullyism." Unable to do much active persecuting themselves, they find their satisfaction in whatever at the moment represents them, whether it be the Ku Klux Klan or Senator McCarthy.

Sometimes, instead of directing charges at individuals, people with this mentality will make more general charges, stating over and over again that the government — or some of our free institutions, such as the schools — are " full of Communists." The basis of this belief is not anything

that could pass for information but rather an emotional
need to believe it, perhaps so as to justify an attitude towards the government — or towards the institution in question — which otherwise would be insupportable.   The
charge is therefore made without ever becoming specific; or
if, under pressure, names are named, they are not the names
of Communists.

It frequently happens that such people feel driven to
make these charges as arguments for their viewpoint in
letters that they write.   A lady wrote me such a letter not
long since, imploring me to believe that because I am a
preacher, I have no understanding of the evil that has
come upon us.   She herself, she said, could name Communists who were working for the government.   I wrote her
back immediately.   My reply was that if she could name
Communists who were working for the government, it was
her duty to inform the FBI; but that if she was making reckless charges, she was damaging her country's welfare.   In
that case, it was *my* duty to inform the FBI — which I did
that afternoon, suggesting that if the lady's claim was false,
she should herself be investigated.

Actually, all who make such claims should be investigated.   What they are doing is not in the least proof of
patriotism but only of malice — or, at best, of emotional
disorder; and it is behavior that transgresses the entire
spirit of the American founding principles.

In the climate of fear now prevailing, however, allegiance
to the founding principles is not the test of patriotism.

"The End of the Road for Some People"

One of the most tragic aspects of this unavowed renunciation of traditional American principles is the havoc

wrought in the lives of those whose loyalty — by the new standards — comes under suspicion. Twice within a month, I have looked into the despairing eyes of men who were contemplating suicide. It is useless to talk to people in this condition as one would to a normal person. Long periods of brooding and anxiety have undermined their health — both physical and mental — and they are oppressed incessantly by fear for the future.

Here, for instance, is a man who has been " under suspicion" for more than a year. He now lives in a world that, for him, is an unceasing nightmare, so that even in matters in which, to an objective mind, his innocence is beyond doubt, he himself has come to feel guilty. It is a familiar condition to psychiatrists — and even more familiar, one conjectures, in the prisons of the Soviet Union and its satellites. After having seen something of this condition in Americans under investigation, I now see that the Communists do not need to resort to drugs or physical torture to wring confessions from their victims. If guilt is imputed for long enough in the presence of unceasing anxiety and fear, the person subjected to the ordeal will absorb guilt into his conscience and it may completely undermine him.

But to return to the man in question. Many years ago in a Western State, he had belonged to an informal group that met once a week to discuss economic questions. A few members of the group were Communists. This added to the interest of the discussion. He listened to what they had to say; he read some literature they recommended to him. It never occurred to him that Communists were conspirators, or that there was anything wicked in associating with them. They had not convinced him of their doctrines but he thought them stimulating. As he understood it, an

American was free to consider all viewpoints and to decide for himself which of them was most persuasive.

During his membership in this group, a public event occurred which aroused his indignation. It seemed to him that the powers of government had been used lawlessly and he engaged in an activity which was intended to redress the injury by appealing to public opinion. So did some Communists.

Later, he went to a meeting where most of those present were Communists; whether it was a Party meeting he did not know; he attended it from curiosity. At the meeting he met a young woman in whom he became interested, and she involved him, over a period of about three months, in various occasions connected with the Communist Party and tried to get him to become a member. This he was unable to do because his viewpoint was increasingly opposed to Communism. He also discovered facts about the young lady which ended her attraction for him.

After leaving the West, he lost touch with his Communist friends, married and settled down in a metropolitan city. Much troubled by the rise of Hitler, he worked in some anti-fascist organizations without knowing that they were controlled by Communists. During the war, he served for two years in one of the United States armed forces, then came to Washington to work for the government.

At the routine inquiry, he answered the usual questions but did not disclose his Communist associations in the West. Since he had never joined the Party nor held Communist opinions, it seemed to him that those incidents of his early life were trivial.

But when he was investigated and called to account, he saw that a formidable case had been made out against him. The question, for instance, as to whether he had ever considered joining the Communist Party had to be answered in the affirmative, since he had in fact considered it although there was never any real possibility that he would have joined it. It was the same with other questions. His Communist friends in the discussion group had seemed to him agreeable and interesting people, and although he now assumed that they were part of a conspiracy, he could not remember that they ever seemed so when he knew them.

Gradually, as the investigation proceeded, he came to have feelings of guilt and disgrace. Probing back into the past, he wondered whether he had done wrong without seeing that it was wrong, or whether his memory had skipped over something culpable. His relationship with the young Communist woman in the West, as he now broodingly reviewed it, became an almost crippling complication. He felt sure of nothing.

It was obvious that this man would not make a good impression upon his investigators. He had become almost sick with apprehension and it showed in his bearing. Yet, his story, as I slowly drew it from him, checking repeatedly to see if discrepancies developed, was entirely straightforward. People in extremity do not lie to a minister. This was the truth.

He was not yet dismissed but sure that it was coming. When it came — or if, without waiting for it, he resigned "under charges" — there was no hope, he felt, of getting a position elsewhere. Wherever he went, his loyalty would be doubted and no employer would take a chance on him. He had very little money. But he had a fair amount of life insurance. If he went on living, he would be nothing but a burden to his family, so why should he not end it now and his family would at least have the insurance?

"Nothing is going to clear things up for me," he said. "It will just go on and on. This business is the end of the road for some people, and I'm one of them."

To the reader who has not passed through this man's experience, the thought of suicide as the solution of his dilemma may seem unthinkable. But it might not seem so if, day after day, for a long period, he had lived with fear and uncertainty; and if, evening by evening, he had endlessly discussed the situation with his wife and found the answer more and more elusive; and if, night by night, he had slept at last with the aid of sleeping tablets, only to wake up in the early morning hours and brood despairingly until the time had come to begin another fretful and anxiety-ridden day.

I can understand that this man's investigators did not have an easy task. Probably, they could never have resolved their indecision, and would therefore have given the government rather than the man the benefit of the "reasonable doubt." It is the climate of fear that is to blame — the miasmic hysteria incited by charlatans and demagogues masquerading as super-patriots.

This man was loyal. He had never been a Communist and never *could* have been. His only "crime" was an open mind and a willingness to discover for himself whatever would help him in forming his opinions. He hated injustice and tyranny. For that reason, he had joined the "front" organizations to help in the fight against Hitler. As a member of the armed services, his part in the fight became literal. He would have fought with equal zeal against the armies of the Kremlin. He was a loyal American.

But he was also of very sensitive temperament, introspective, rather finely balanced emotionally. In my study, he could make his case clear, and I could go back over his life and relieve him of his irrational feelings of guilt. But when he was back under investigation he made a poor showing.

There will be an occasional reader — just as there are similar people in every audience — who will ask whether I, as a minister, was not imposed upon whereas the investigators were more shrewd. I will not stop to try to convey to such a person what it means to have spent many years looking into the inwardness of human life, or how little cause there would be, in the security of a minister's study, to deceive the person to whom you had come for help. It is sufficient to say that this man did not come to me hoping that I could do something to assist him in his investigation; he came to discover whether I could find reasons why he should not commit suicide.

Actually, of course, people are seldom dissuaded from suicide by logic; they are warmed by human sympathy, built up in self-esteem, lightened of their burdens, made to feel the contagion of hope, restored by degrees to their former faith in life and in their own power to cope with it.

" It's the end of the road for some people," this man had said in his despair. And in some cases — an unknown number — that is what it has proved to be. In this particular instance, courage came back and the road opened up again. But why should it ever have closed? If the persecutors and man-hunters who are making headlines and wrecking human lives had met with more resistance from responsible, decent citizens when they began to sow mistrust and inflame the base passions that light the fires of persecution, it could not have happened at all.

" It's the end of the road for some people " — such words could have a wider application!   If the senseless and obsessional phobias about Communism in America are allowed to divide and weaken us so that we are unable to contend adequately with Communism where it is really threatening us — aggressive Communism abroad — it could be the end of the road for more people than have ever perished at one time since history began, and perhaps the end of the road for America.

" *What Does a Decent Person Do?* "

But to turn again to some of the consequences of living in a climate of fear, I must confess that I had often felt puzzled by the frequency with which witnesses before Congressional Committees took refuge in the " self-incrimination clause " of the Fifth Amendment.   They refused to answer questions, that is to say, because the answer would " tend to incriminate or degrade " them, and in this refusal they have the protection of the law.   It is certainly a wise provision, just as Congressional immunity is a wise provision, but both can be abused.

My assumption was — and for the most part still is — that a person who refuses to say whether he is or ever was a Communist is thereby admitting to the fact just as much as if he said " Yes."   But I have discovered that this is not so in all cases.

For example, a man came to see me on the day before he was due to appear at a Committee hearing.   He had heard me say what I have just stated above — or had read it — and felt an obligation to enlighten me. He was going to plead the " self-incrimination clause " right from the beginning of the hearing.

" Then you either are or have been a Communist," I said. " No," he replied, " that's what I want you to understand. I am not now and have never been a Communist, but I have associated with Communists."

" Why not say so? " I asked.

" I will tell you," he said. " I have been over all this with my lawyer several times. I hate to plead the Fifth Amendment, but that's what I have to do. If I respond to the questioning, they will ask me for the names of the Communists I knew. Now, the fact is that most of those people are no longer Communists and wish to God they had never touched the Communist Party with a ten-foot pole. They are perfectly loyal Americans. But if their names are mentioned, their employers will dismiss them. In the present hysteria, they could scarcely do anything else. And I can't have that on my conscience.

" Maybe you don't know how hard it is to leave the Communist Party," he continued. " They get after you — I mean the Party people do — and write anonymous letters and call up on the telephone and tell your friends and the people where you work that you are a Communist. If you once survive this and get somewhere far enough away from where they can hurt you, you sure hope that you can put it all behind you. Well, that is why I won't name their names. They have families. They would be ruined. I'm not going to do that to them no matter what happens."

" Couldn't you just tell the Committee what you have told me? " I asked.

He shook his head. "They could go back over the record and identify them — or some of them. Say just one word and they have you where they want you. There are several of them up there on the dais, all trying to trip you up. That's what they want to do — trap you! It's five or six to one. I couldn't be sure of coming through. My lawyer says the one safe way is to plead the Fifth Amendment. Then the hearing is short and no damage is done to anybody but yourself. Tell me. What else can a decent person do? What would you do, yourself?"

"If you really want me to answer that question," I replied, "I will. But I would like to say first that I understand your difficulty. And of course, I am not in your situation. For myself, I would never plead the ' self-incrimination clause '; I would just explain that my conscience did not permit me to do damage to good people whom I knew to be loyal."

"They could cite you for contempt," he interjected.

"Yes, they could," I admitted. "And that would be all right with me. I would fight them in the courts, fight them in the newspapers, fight them from my pulpit. I would never yield my conscience into their keeping, and I believe that sooner or later, public opinion would sustain me."

My visitor smiled at me a little wanly. I realized what was coming. "I couldn't afford the courts, I couldn't get space in the newspapers, and I don't have a pulpit," he said, all in one breath.

There was nothing left for me to say. After he had gone, I repeated his question over and over, "What can a decent person do?"

"You Lose Some of Your Humanity"

One of the most difficult tasks in counselling people who
have been unjustly treated in the various investigations is
the dispelling of bitterness. What do you say to a young
woman, a " second-generation " American who had insisted
in an argument with friends that not all Communists were
bad since some of her own family (in a country now behind the Iron Curtain) called themselves Communists, and
who was reported and asked to explain her views under
suspicion of disloyalty? She was absolutely unable to believe that her family and friends whom she knew and loved
had suddenly become altogether evil. Yet, she never for
a moment was attracted to Communism. Her conflict was
between her actual experience of her family, which she was
unable to distort into a false judgment, and the present
notion of what a person may think and say and still be
counted loyal. She had taken quite literally the great
American principles of tolerance and freedom of expression.
She had supposed that she would be treated in accordance
with them.

The goodness of her character was as transparent as the
honesty of her mind. She was entirely without guile. Far
more than most people, she could be trusted. Yet, her
loyalty was in question. How does one convey to such a
person that the United States is still a good country and
most of its people just and kind? How can she be persuaded that the traditional American principles really mean
what they say?

Moreover, she was making a valuable point. If a time
never comes when there is enough goodness in the people
who at present are Communist, to make it possible for

them to reject the evils of Communism and join with the rest of us in building a secure and peaceful world, we are all doomed together and mankind will go down to destruction.

I asked someone in the government service what possible justification there was for persecuting this young woman. In reply, he told me of other cases, and of the fear that prevented people who knew better from coming to the defense of those who were being unjustly treated. "After a while," he said, "you feel that you are losing some of your humanity."

The words startled me. They were the same I had used in describing an experience in Hitler's Germany and another in Czechoslovakia. I had been sitting with some friends, one of them German, in a side-walk cafe in Berlin late on a summer evening in the 1930's. Suddenly I was aware of a commotion in the street. I looked out and saw two brown-shirts dragging a Jewish boy down the side-walk and hitting and kicking him. Instinctively, I felt myself rising from my chair, only to be plunged back into it by my German friend. "For God's sake," he said, "you can't do anything. And if you think your American passport will protect you, think of me!"

He was right. There was nothing I could do — except perhaps get my friend into trouble. But I felt that I had lost some of my humanity. I had witnessed cruelty and done nothing to hinder it. I had seen evil just an arm's length away and my arm had not gone out. This was what it meant to live in Hitler's Germany. You lost some of your humanity.

Again, in Prague, in February of 1948, where I was the guest of Jan Masaryk (but never saw him) during the week the Communists seized Czechoslovakia. The plane that was to take me to Paris was on the run-way, warming up the engines, when a truck came across the airport and presently a ladder was raised and the door of the airplane opened, and two uniformed men came in. They looked at each of us in turn, finally recognized the man they wanted, and took him away. I, as an American, watched the proceeding with misgiving and followed it from beginning to end. I had not learned to be afraid. But the others on the plane looked through the portholes, buried themselves in their newspapers, turned to anything whatever rather than see what was happening.

It was safest not to have seen! If you were questioned later, you had seen *nothing!* Nothing whatever unusual. No, you had been looking through the porthole, waiting for the plane to take off. Again, I felt the sickening feeling that I was losing some of my humanity. Could such things happen and there be no protest? Was it thus that civilization and its values leaked away?

And now, I had heard the same words spoken in America. How far could it go — this evil thing? Americans, too, were afraid. What hope was there anywhere if the most privileged people on earth, with the brightest promise known to history, were losing their humanity?

PART ONE

THE MODERN PREDICAMENT

1. Recurrence of an Ancient Malady

The twentieth century began in optimism. A new era had been inaugurated in which the evils that had darkened the past were no longer possible. "Man's inhumanity to man" was nearly over; tyranny and oppression were rapidly receding; enlightenment and progress were firmly established; the time had come to "ring out the old, ring in the new"; the modern world was on its way.

In spite of the harshness of events, this mood of confidence has been slow to yield to the realities. The First World War, dismaying though it was in its destructiveness and carnage, was regarded as the death throes of the ancient order; because of it, mankind would proceed that much more swiftly towards consolidating the gains that had been made, and through the League of Nations would gird the world with unassailable security. The Russian Revolution, with its terrors and atrocities, could not endure; when its early, violent phase was over, it would settle down into a peaceful, gradual reformation.

It was not until the rise of Hitler that the confidence of the new era was seriously shaken. The fascism of Mussolini had seemed boisterous rather than barbaric: a product of the aftermath of war, solely Italian and doubtless transitional. Democracy, when it returned, would work better in a well-disciplined nation. After all, there could be no progress without change, and change at first might move in wrong directions. In due time, it would right itself. There was little to fear in Mussolini.

Thus optimism, blind to the early indications of a dimming prospect, reasserted itself. Hitler, however, a self-declared barbarian who had become the master of a great nation, could not be brushed aside. He had achieved power by appealing to the lowest level of human motivation and was in revolt against civilization itself. He had a numerous following which applauded his barbarity. It was therefore evident that, at least in Germany, one of the most advanced of modern nations, the evils of the past were recurring in the present and were threatening to possess the future.

With the defeat of Hitler at incalculable cost, it was hoped that barbarism had been finally suppressed, and that once again there would be room for optimism. The nightmare had ended. Hitler, with his gas chambers, his racism, his brutal massacres, his vicious propaganda, had been vanquished. The United Nations would succeed where the League of Nations had failed. Its structure was more realistic. The great powers, whatever their differences, were weary of war. They would enforce security.

Then came the disclosure that the dynamics of Communism — which many supposed had been redirected during the alliance of the " peace-loving nations " towards co-operation with the Western democracies — were entirely unchanged. Communism, like Nazism, was a revolt against civilization. The Soviet Union, as a result of the war, was immensely more powerful, the aggressive center of a world conspiracy. Once again, those who had wished to be hopeful of the future were compelled to reckon with resurgent barbarism: slave camps and torture, assassination and massacre, persecution and terror. Inhumanity had not been banished: it must be faced anew in Communism.

Not that these evils had waited for the defeat of Nazism before they began to appear in Communism. They had been there from the beginning. But when Kremlin aggression and conspiracy, during the latter part of the war and after its conclusion, brought one nation after another under Communist domination, it became plainer than before what the aims of Communism were, and by what means Communists intended to achieve them. No longer was it a matter of reports of " liquidations " and " purges " within Russia, with conflicting interpretations of their import; it was reliable knowledge of brutal despotism in extended areas and of constant, unremitting persecution.

Nor were the despots always Russian or the persecutors officials of the Soviet Union. Persons of any nationality and of widely differing traditions, in embracing Communism, absorbed its evil, accepted its standards, and adopted its patterns of behavior. Moreover, as Hitler and his following demonstrated, these perversions of civilized values were not solely Communist. They could express themselves equally as well in a fascist movement as in Communism. A Communist could become a Nazi, or a Nazi a Communist, with very little change in motivation and none at all in moral character. The fact is that in the revolt against civilization which these movements channel and facilitate, the sanction may be ideological but the source is always psychological; the motivation can be attached to any theory or program, Marxist or other, which rebels against established values and surrenders civilized restraints.

It is thus apparent that the evil in human nature which created these movements is not bounded by them. It could create new movements, antagonistic to existing ones and with announced aims contrived to deceive the unwary. It could create a movement violently opposed to Communism, as Nazism was, but in its real nature it would resemble Communism. That is to say, it would be tyrannous, brutal, contemptuous of human rights, aggressive, conspiratorial, falsely-accusing, bold with the 'big lie,' quick to persecute — and in short, no matter what its outer form, its inner character would be that of Communism. Thus, the basic threat is not the movement in which the revolt against civilization is organized, but the revolt itself. Hence, besides resisting Communism and any resurgence that may occur of Nazism or fascism, we must be alert to new expressions of the same dark passions that created these movements.

The truth is that our earlier optimism was false. We mistook a favorable interval in history for a permanent advance. The evil in human nature which fed the flames of persecution and oppression in the past, far from being banished, or exceptional in cases such as Germany or Russia, is present everywhere. It can be incited, not only by Communism and Nazism, fascism and falangism, but by appeals of any kind to fear and malice. A nation such as the United States or Britain, with long experience in restraint and tolerance, and well-established traditions of respect for human rights, may be more resistant to it than authoritarian countries; but no nation is immune.

In the United States, there is already cause for alarm. The fears of an anxious and uneasy populace, deprived of its security in isolation and compelled to face, unexpectedly and unwillingly, the problems of a world in jeopardy, are being exploited by power-hungry adventurers who claim to be defending the country from the threat of Communism. Actually, they are doing the opposite: they are weakening the country by spreading fear and mistrust and by falsely accusing those who believe that progressive democracy is the true alternative to Communism. To the mind of any rational observer, it is plain that the country is being defended against Communism by its armed forces, its agencies of law enforcement, and its citizens who can out-think the Communists in creative planning and enlightened policies. But these adventurers are not appealing to rationality. They are appealing to fear and frustration, resentment and malevolence.

The success or failure of their appeal will be determined by the American people, who must decide whether they wish to face the dangers which beset them with courage and sanity, or yield to the fear and folly which would prove their undoing.

Admittedly, the strain is great, and in times of stress people do strange things: useless, unavailing things, like a drowning man grasping at a straw. He knows that it will not keep him afloat but his hand goes out compulsively. If anyone attempts to rescue him, he is likely to add to the danger. Instead of co-operating intelligently, which requires restraint and the guidance of reason, he acts instinctively. If he is physically strong and his rescuer unwary, both of them may go down together — because the drowning man is controlled by panic and cannot bring himself to let go.

It is much the same with other sorts of panic. People who feel themselves threatened by events may give up trying to reason and act upon impulse. This can mean not only that what they do is futile, but also that it is cruel and serves no purpose but the relief of embittered feelings or the venting of anger. Sometimes a man who is disappointed or frustrated will kick his dog who is devoted to him, or start a quarrel with his wife who loves him. When things go wrong there is an instinctive wish to find someone to blame it upon: someone, if possible, too helpless to defend himself. This same motivation can cause a nation, or a large part of it, to persecute innocent people. It is a sickness — in psychological terms, quite literally a sickness — and a very ancient one.

It was this sickness that Hitler exploited in the German people while they were suffering from a severe depression, following a war in which they were defeated. He played upon their feeling of humiliation, their exasperation at being helpless, their belief that they had deserved better fortune, and their hatred of their enemies. He turned their resentment, first in this direction, then in that: but he always came back to the Jews. Thus a nation of civilized people, or a considerable part of it, became persecutors of the falsely accused — and in the process were subdued to the designs of Hitler.

There are, of course, other motivations besides these that lead to persecution and open the way to tyranny. Later, we shall consider them. But they all arise from the untamed impulses in human nature which, in century after century, have withered the promise that civilized mankind would build the world that its prophets had heralded and its poets dreamed.

A society, like an individual, can become sick of soul. Indeed, we must never forget that societies are composed of individuals and that nothing whatever that happens can happen otherwise than because individuals have willed it or permitted it. If the individuals of a society are morally sick, evil aims will overcome the good. If they are bitter and resentful because events are thwarting them, they invite this sickness; if they are wrapped up in selfish aims and determined to be deaf to the cry of the world for wider justice and broader purposes and deeper sympathy, they are sure to become afflicted with it. Repeatedly in history, it has happened that, under stress, the good in human nature has surrendered to the evil, but this can never happen in the mass except by happening to individuals. When it does, the moral health of the society is unequal to the strain upon it, and it soon succumbs to the inhumanities of persecution — swiftly followed by the brutalities of tyranny and the humiliations of servitude.

But it begins with sickness of the soul. The psychologists would call it a mass neurosis, or perhaps, if it is bad enough, a national psychosis. Yet, they too would recognize that what happens to the mass can do so only through its individuals. We should be attentive to the psychologists; they have much to teach us. But we should also see that a moral sickness carries with it moral responsibility. This is not a malady which comes like an epidemic of physical sickness and which we do not know how to avoid. If we are afflicted with it, we have willed it so, if only by default.

What it would do to us is not in doubt. We have recalled what it did in Hitler's Germany; we have seen it at work in Communism; we must learn to recognize it in our own society before it is too late.

2. The World Nobody Wants

It is not unnatural that an age which had taken for granted the brightness of its own promise should find it difficult to face the new, unhappy world of insecurity. To Americans particularly, the change is unaccountable — as though spring, instead of turning into summer, had gone back into winter and the earth was snow-covered in July. As well as trusting in their isolation from the Old World and its quarrels, Americans had come to think that progress was as certain in human society as it was in automotive design, and that mankind, to use a favorite phrase, was moving " onward and upward forever."

It has thus been hard, especially for Americans, to understand that modern optimism was not soundly based, and that the twentieth century, despite its sanguine mood, had not repealed the laws of history. The difficulty is partly due, no doubt, to the misconceptions by which the popular view of history is colored. " The past is prologue," we were told, and if anyone asked, " Prologue to what?," his attention was called to the skyscraper, the gasoline engine, the airplane, the radio set, the vitamin tablet, and Miss America of the current year. Dazzled by our own inventiveness, we had not considered that ingenuity may not have made us wiser, or that air-conditioning cannot save us from the fate of Nineveh and Tyre.

We knew that earlier civilizations were also sometimes

confident, but we thought that they had fallen because man was not yet inventive enough, or organized enough, or enterprising enough to find solutions for his problems. The highly productive, efficiently organized, boldly enterprising modern age was different and would prove more adequate.

Only recently have we come to doubt this blithe appraisal. Bewilderedly, we have looked afresh at our inventiveness, wondering how long it will be before we make an atom bomb that can burn off the earth's atmosphere; shudderingly, we have seen to what evil purpose large societies can be organized by tyrants; in dazed frustration, we have watched the ever-growing enterprise of making war more suicidal; and when our foremost historian, Arnold Toynbee, calmly informs us that after our civilization has been destroyed, the Negrito Pygmies of Central Africa may salvage "some fraction" of its values and apply their "unexpectedly pure" religion to giving mankind a new and more promising beginning,[1] we are no longer shocked and incredulous but merely wretched. It might come true.

We are ceasing to be optimists, but not enough of us, as yet, are beginning to be realists. Too many among us, instead of looking upon the new face of reality with a steady gaze, determined to discover how courage and wisdom can be made to contend with it, turn away in petulance to nurse their disappointments and frustrations.

Such people are not to be blamed, of course, for not liking perils and disagreeable conditions. No sane person would wish for our present situation. Nevertheless, it is our real situation, the one in which we are actually and

---

[1] Arnold J. Toynbee, *Civilization on Trial* (London: Oxford University Press, 1948), p. 162.

inexorably involved, and its conditions can only be changed for the better if we are courageous enough to cope with them in terms of reality. To lose our nerve, give way to fear, become fretful and resentful, is to sap the strength we need for tasks that cannot be evaded.

It is this emotional state that political adventurers find it so easy to prey upon. Unhappy people, frustrated and discontented, readily respond to the demagoguery that invites them to find targets for their wrath in fellow-citizens who have done no more to bring the present evils upon us than have the rest of us. The urge to persecute, which unfortunately is never far below the surface, is stirred up by those who hope that it will carry them to power — men with perverse emotional hungers and distorted personalities, who, like Hitler and the Communist tyrannizers, thrive on persecution.

If we are to win our way out of a world that nobody wants into a better, happier world in which we can be secure and hopeful, it must be through realism and the patient use of reason; our situation will never be remedied by an emotional debauch.

It is never, of course, an easy thing to appeal to reason. Today, it is less so than ever. The common assumption has been that people could be made to believe anything — and to act upon it — by appealing to the emotional. They are to be swayed, not by argument but by assertion. They are subdued, not by logic but by the numbing influence of reiteration.

" This coffee is the one good coffee because it is the one good coffee in a thousand advertisements." " This lotion will cure your dandruff because the same luxurious head of hair has been portrayed in all the shiny-paper magazines concurrently." "This cigarette will be a solace to your throat because, no matter how much you cough when smoking it, there is a picture of a white-jacketed physician on the printed matter that promotes it."

" Eat these cornflakes and feel like Hercules! " " Read this book and be as serene as Marcus Aurelius! " " Try our home-cooked food in this five-hundred seat restaurant! " " Take a course of public speaking at the Put-Yourself-Over Institute and talk like William Jennings Bryan in eleven weeks! " " Learn from us how to win friends and influence people and be a power like John L. Lewis every time you raise your eyebrows! "

Even religion is not exempt. " Come to church and get God on your side. Our combination of Bible teaching and popular psychology can do it for you painlessly: no danger whatever of your conscience being disturbed."

What wonder is it that the big lie is so successful a technique when we have lived so long in the world of the boldly false assertion? What chance does reason have with people who are inured to being manipulated by emotion?

The answer is that no matter how debilitated the rational side of our life may be, we must have recourse to reason in our present circumstances or be herded down the path to degradation and defeat. The present world, no matter how little we like it, is the world we must live in — if it is not destroyed by war — for a long time to come. Repeatedly, situations will arise that the inflamers of dark passions can use to turn us away from the struggle with our real enemy and provoke enmities among ourselves and against our allies. By one course or another, this would bring us to disaster. To prevent it, we must refuse to be manipulated by those who use discontentment to promote dissension; we must give our attention to an intelligent and courageous reckoning with the conditions we must change if the world is ever again to be happy or secure.

These conditions include not only Communist aggressiveness and the need for continued military strength; they include, also, the poverty and destitution against which multitudes who were once resigned and passive are now rebelling; they include race consciousness and the aspirations of once backward populations to achieve nationhood and freedom; they include all the claims that a world in ferment is making upon the more advanced, more fortunate nations. We are competing with the Communists for leadership in these areas of upheaval. It is urgent that our own free way of life and not Communist subjection shall prevail in these contested, undecided areas. We cannot afford the loss of them to Communism.

No matter how much we wish that the world made fewer demands upon us, this is the world as it is and these the demands that must be met. We must face realities. We must give up the childishness of being discontented and resentful. We must recognize as leaders, not those who pander to our lowest motives but those who tell us the truth about the world, and ask us to understand it sympathetically. Only the highest motives will prove good enough for the tasks before us.

3. Who Is to Blame?

The notion that, when a society is involved in a misfortune, a "scape-goat" must be found and made to suffer for it, is a very old one. It was in this way that primitive peoples appeased the gods who were thought to have decreed their misfortune. But it was also in this way that they found relief for their emotional tensions. Any feeling the society may have had that it was being penalized for wrong-doing was abated by imputing the guilt to the scape-goat.

The irrationality of this practice is obvious; but emotionally, it is still satisfying to those who have not yet outgrown the primitiveness which civilization often hides but seldom effaces. Hitler succeeded in making the Jews the scape-goat for the misfortunes of Germany. The Communists have had a succession of scape-goats — some of them surprising choices as viewed from the outer world, but to the Communists themselves, no doubt, entirely appropriate to the exigency.

In the United States, when it was apparent that victory in the Second World War had gone chiefly to the Russians, and that instead of security and "normalcy" there had emerged a "cold war" and the encroachments of Communism, it was felt that there must be those — other than the Russians — who were to blame. This was partly, as we shall see in the next chapter, because of the illusion that American power is all-decisive and therefore must have been used in some way — or misused — to bring about the post-war situation. But it was also because of the morbid need to find a scape-goat. Things had gone wrong — very wrong; who were the culprits?

The real culprits, of course, were Stalin and his men of the Kremlin. But they were inaccessible; only through war, if at all, could they be made available. There must be culprits in America, men who had bungled, or, still worse, had treacherously contrived the post-war situation. There must be others who had encouraged it, perhaps sympathizers with the Russians, secret Communists and fellow-travellers.

Now, there was this much fact in that belief: there really was — and is — a Communist conspiracy within the United States. There truly are Americans who have been traitors. It is plain, for instance, that the Soviet Union, by the use of American agents, acquired atomic information of extreme importance. There are doubtless Communist plans, in case of war, for widespread sabotage. The belief of the American people that Communism was dangerous within the United States had a substantial basis.

But there was no real basis for believing that there were Americans who had contrived the post-war situation for the benefit of the Russians. There were indeed mistakes of policy, but these were not acts of treason; and in any case, the policy represented, at the time, the wishes of the American people. Nor was it sound to suppose that all who had been friendly to Russia during the war or earlier, and who had hoped that the Soviet Union would collaborate peacefully with the Western democracies, were to blame for what actually happened, or were attached to one extent or another to the Communist conspiracy.

The persecutors of these people — or of those they single out to be condemned — have created a climate of opinion in which an American citizen, to prove his loyalty, must show that he was never at any time hopeful in his estimation of Communism and that he had never believed for a moment that a Communist could be anything but evil.

The Congressional committees have forgotten that Congress itself was once hopeful of Communism — so recklessly hopeful that it demobilized our armies in Europe immediately after the war was ended, thus leaving the Soviet Union free to dominate Poland, keep Germany divided, seize control of Czechoslovakia and do everything else that the dissolution of our armed might invited and encouraged. If this breakneck demobilization was not based upon the confidence that Communists were to be trusted — at least in making and maintaining a just peace — the members who pressed for it should be tried for treason. More than any other one thing, it was this action of Congress that paved the way for Soviet aggression. Not only did it physically remove the military deterrent to Communist aims which, until then, the United States had possessed in Europe, but it made clear to the Kremlin that the United States was so bent upon a headlong flight into "normalcy" that Communist planners had little to fear. Provided they avoided extreme provocation, the atom bomb, the sole effective weapon of the United States in the period when no other country had it, would never be used.

If, therefore, Congress took this action believing that Communists were utterly evil and on no account to be trusted, the Congressmen concerned were traitors. If, on the other hand, Congress believed that the Russians, though Communists, were trustworthy and would join us in ending aggression and building international security, Congress was more pitifully deceived than any erstwhile fellow-traveller who ever stood before a Congressional committee.

The truth is, of course, that Congressmen as much as all others — indeed, more than many others — were slow to recognize the threat of Communism. It was a mistake of judgment so egregious, and so grave in its consequences, that one would think that a Committeeman would blush to mention the trivial errors of the Committee's persecuted victims.[2]

What should be recognized is that the people who joined organizations that expressed friendship towards Russia, or which, in other ways, were hopeful of Communism, did not do so because they were pro-Communist but because they were pro-humanity. They wanted to believe that Communists at least were working for international security. They thought that Communism, if it was not too sharply repelled, might change for the better. They hoped that Russia, when the revolutionary phase had

---

[2] It may be pertinent to mention that the present writer publicly protested against the rash demobilization of our armed forces in Europe at the time when it occurred. He did not expect that the Communists would keep faith with us. But the considerable number of letters which his protest brought him were all critical of his position, and some of them denounced him as a militarist, which he most certainly was not. All he wanted was a settlement which was just and would last, instead of a situation inviting aggression and threatening still a further generation with a disastrous world war. The point to be emphasized is not that his judgment happened to be correct but that Americans of all shades of political opinion were virtually unanimous in demanding immediate demobilization. The Congress, of course, demanded it in response to political pressure from its constituencies. But it is shameless and hypocritical for Congressional committees to blame individual citizens for being deceived by Communism when Congress itself was as much deceived as anybody.

spent itself, would become a genuine democracy. They believed that Stalin, if he could be assured that we had no aggressive intentions towards Russia, such as we had at the end of the First World War, would co-operate in building world peace. These were vain hopes as it turned out, but not unworthy ones. It would have been far better for the world if they had proved sound. Is there anyone so foolish or so wicked as to wish that Russia will always be an enemy and that peace will never be possible?

It is neither a crime against the State nor a sin against God to have faith in human nature, and it was out of this faith that these people who were hopeful of Communism — with a very few deplorable exceptions — felt moved to take an optimistic view. Those of us who were more skeptical were not for that reason morally superior. We merely, for one reason or another, were more correct in our judgment. After all, there is no evil in trying to foster peace, or in believing in tolerance and co-operation, or in seeking a world unity that would give security to civilization.

It is wicked to blame people for believing desperately that there is good in all human nature, even in that of Communists. Their mistakes were not of motive but of judgment. Anyone who takes action makes some mistakes; and this is just as true of people who are working for human welfare as of anyone else. The persecutors of these people were not devoted to human welfare as much as they were to narrower and more selfish aims; so they never ventured into anything in which they could have made this kind of mistake. This is not, however, because they understood the threat of Communism. It is because they were against anything, and still are, that promises a wider justice and a better life for the common people — and they are not quite certain, even now, that Communism does not hold that promise.

It is because they still have this belief, or half-belief, that they are against Communism but not much disturbed by Franco's Spain — and, in the past, were slow to see the danger in Mussolini and the evil in Hitler. One hesitates to judge; it is well to keep in mind the contradictions and complexities of human nature. Yet, one entertains the thought that the persecuting committeemen are fearful that there may be good in Communism. Similar-minded men believed there might be good in Hitler and were sure there was in Mussolini. Those who are truly against tyranny are against *all* tyranny. They are unwilling to be tyrannical themselves. The comparison, therefore, between the persecutors and the persecuted is very much to the advantage of the latter. Their motives were worthy, their intention was above reproach. They made mistakes only of judgment, and it is sad for the world that they were not right. If matters had turned out as they expected, we would not have had to fight in Korea. Instead of re-arming — and needing far greater military preparations than we are, in fact, making — we would now be building for peace. Is there anyone, fair-minded enough to recall the actual situation during the war and in the years immediately following, who considers that these people deserve to be blamed?

We are not thinking — and this should be obvious — of actual Communists, working under party discipline, who gained control of organizations devoted to human welfare, or who perfidiously announced worthy aims for organizations they had themselves created to serve their own conspiratorial ends, or who distorted the policies of progressive movements with the intention of bringing discredit upon them. Communist conspirators who engaged in these activities are traitors not only to their country but to all humanity. They perverted the goodness the world so sorely needs and turned it into evil.

Nor are we thinking of the pro-Communists who, without being members of the Party, consciously fostered the Party's aims. We are thinking only of that far more numerous group which, for a while, had hope that the Soviet Union which had suffered so much from Hitler would join the rest of us in building and maintaining peace; and who thought, perhaps, that Communists, being people, would learn as other people did to correct their mistakes and arrive at a higher level. These people, whether in the Government or just ordinary citizens, deserve no blame for their motivation. Yet, they are the ones most persecuted.

The truth is — and the sooner the better we arrive at it — we are *all* to blame in one degree or another for our present predicament. Almost the entire population of the United States is to blame — if anyone at all may be blamed — for throwing away our chance to make a just settlement following the war; for that is what was done when immediate demobilization was demanded.

Similarly, almost the entire population of the United States is to blame for believing that the Communist tyrants would co-operate in creating a system of security. Those who did not rely upon this as much as they did upon our sole possession of the atom bomb are to blame — if anybody is — for the vanity of supposing that we alone could make such a bomb, when it was well known that the bomb was made possible by the work of foreign scientists more than of our own and we had been told that Russia had secured the services of similar scientists.

But there are other and wider considerations. How is

blame to be apportioned for the restlessness of Asia? It began before the Communists had any influence upon it, and would be there if Communism had never existed. Who is to be blamed for the fearful destructiveness of the new weapons? The scientists developed them only because they were fearful that the enemy would do so first. To have prevented their development, the world would have needed to be more secure and settled after the First World War; but what did we, the people of the United States, do to improve international security and promote a settlement? What did we do to arrest the rise of Hitler? What use did we make of the warnings so solemnly given us a decade earlier by President Wilson?

But then, how far back must we go? And to what end? Of what use is it looking for someone to blame? Mistakes of many kinds have been made by all of us. We need humility to improve our comprehensions of each other and unity in the face of a resourceful and persistent enemy. It is childish — worse than that, it is cruel and barbarous — to seek scape-goats for the sins of an entire community. What we need is to recognize the mistakes we are still making, and while there is time, correct them.

The American people are essentially fair-minded and capable of adult thinking and civilized behavior. This is the time to be reminded of it. Seeking someone to blame is a primitive procedure and persecution is senseless fanaticism. To cope successfully with Communism, we must cement our democracy more strongly together, not splinter and divide it into factions. And the cement that we need is sanity.

4. The American Fantasy

The full awakening of the American people to the new, unhappy turn events were taking probably came with the fall of China to the Communists. This was unquestionably a grievous misfortune, and the alarm that was felt about it was justified. But unfortunately, instead of assessing the situation realistically and developing a practical policy to deal with it, many Americans, including political leaders, angrily demanded to be told how such a calamity had been allowed to happen and which Americans were responsible for it.

Now, the fact was — and it was plainly visible to anyone who took the trouble to look at it — that the United States could not have prevented the defeat of Chiang Kai-shek, except perhaps by a full-scale war in China. Even this would very likely have failed, since Russia and China have a convenient common frontier and the supply of the Communist forces would have been easy for the Kremlin, whereas American supply, over great stretches of ocean, would have been next to impossible to maintain. Moreover, very few Americans were willing for such a war, even though they may have thought that we could win it.

Later, there were those who proposed that the Korean War be extended into China — their belief being that this was the only way the Chinese allies of the North Koreans could be defeated. More prudent strategists foresaw that war with China could easily assume a magnitude that would drain the United States of men and material without significantly weakening Russia. The Kremlin would then be free to conquer Europe, and Americans would have no means of preventing it.

These were the realities of the situation. But there was little disposition to face realities. Stunned by the fact that China was " lost " to the free world, and incredulous that this could have happened if United States policy had been firmly against it, many Americans, perhaps a majority, began looking for the Americans who were to blame.

If they had gone into this question with sufficient thoroughness, they would have discovered that, to the extent that Americans had contributed to the " loss " of China at all, it was chiefly in the early 1920's that the contribution had been made. In the period immediately following the First World War, the young Chinese intellectuals, who were later to influence the situation so decisively, were devoted to the ideals set forth by President Wilson and their imagination had been fired by what they thought to be the aims of Western democracy. But with the refusal of the United States to join the League of Nations, and the general let-down following the repudiation of Wilsonian idealism, the young Chinese leaders turned to Moscow and the successful Russian Revolution. It was in this way that Communism was introduced into China.[3] If, therefore, Americans must be blamed for what happened later, those most culpable were the isolationists and reactionaries of the 1920's.

[3] See Benjamin I. Schwartz, *Chinese Communism and the Rise of Mao*, Cambridge: Harvard University Press — Carnegie financed report, 1951.

The Chinese Revolution was not begun by the Communists; it had been going on for a long while and might easily have followed the principles of the American Revolution instead of the Russian. But Moscow had a clearer recognition than Washington did of what was involved in the Chinese upheaval and made full use of the opportunity to exploit it. By the end of the Second World War, it was too late for the United States to intervene effectively; the American diplomatic and military missions that were sent to China all failed — not because they did not make an honest effort, but because, by then, there was almost nothing they could do.

The fact to be faced is that the power of the United States, although great, is not unlimited. Many things are happening in the world that Americans cannot prevent. There are more than twice as many Chinese as there are Americans, and they are resolved upon changes which the American people, through wise diplomacy, might influence, but which they could not have forestalled and cannot reverse. It is necessary that we understand this and accept it, or we shall continue to be afflicted with what Professor Dennis W. Brogan, of Cambridge University, England, has called " the illusion of American omnipotence." [4]

This illusion, he reminds us, is " that any situation which distresses or endangers the United States can only exist because some Americans have been fools or knaves." He goes on to show that not only in the case of China but also in Europe, Americans have been perplexed because the American wish has not been fulfilled — the unconscious basis of the perplexity being " the illusion that the world

[4] See his lucid and extremely useful essay under that title, in *Harper's* Magazine for December, 1952.

must go the American way if the Americans want it strongly enough and give firm orders to their agents to see that it is done."

Not only is this illusion damaging to us in international affairs: it is even more damaging within the United States. It is the sanction of the current persecution of government officials, the charge being that, since they had the power of the United States behind them, they must have been bunglers or traitors to fail in doing what they could not possibly have done. Mr. Acheson, for instance, as Secretary of State, was blamed for situations which it is inconceivable that he could have prevented. Being human, and facing problems of immense complexity, it is altogether likely that he did make some mistakes, as every other Secretary of State had done before him. But to assume that he and his predecessors could have controlled the population of China or changed the aims of the Kremlin or rolled back the North Koreans by the fiat of American diplomacy is to attribute to government servants godlike powers which it is absurd and childish to suppose them to possess.

In this attitude, to quote again from Professor Brogan, there is " a curious absence of historical awe and historical curiosity. The Chinese Revolution, an event of immense importance, is often discussed as if it were simply a problem in American foreign and domestic policy and politics. The Communist triumph in China is discussed as if it were simply the result of the mistakes, and worse than mistakes, of General Marshall, Secretary Acheson, President Roosevelt, and the Institute of Pacific Relations; and as if the Communists or the Russians would not have ' captured ' China had American policy been represented and controlled by Representative Judd — or even, perhaps, by Senators Cain and Jenner."

The same attitude of treating other countries as though their affairs were "simply a problem in American foreign and domestic policy and politics" — and particularly "politics" — is manifested in the remarkable mission of Mr. Cohn and Mr. Schine, of Senator McCarthy's Permanent Subcommittee on Investigations, to Europe in the spring of 1953. Upon arriving at the Hotel Excelsior in Munich, for instance, they asked for adjoining but separate rooms, and explained to the bewildered *hofmeister*, "You see, we don't work for the State Department." This remark was reported in all the newspapers of West Germany — and in many other European newspapers besides — the readers of which, when they recovered from their dazed astonishment, were forced to conclude that emissaries of the American Congress, duly accredited by a committee of the Senate, regarded the official agencies of American diplomacy with scorn and contempt. Not only so, but they were assuming that Europeans, as represented by the German citizen to whom they were speaking, must share this feeling. It was necessary to make it clear that the two gentlemen who were making the request were not State Department agents but official Americans who were entitled to respect.

Almost incredibly, the basis upon which Messrs. Cohn and Schine were proceeding was that in the countries they visited it was well understood that the affairs of these countries were primarily "a problem in American politics"; indeed, the two emissaries did not hesitate to seek, from citizens of these countries, information which might assist them in what they regarded as the over-all aim of American policy: namely, victory for Senator McCarthy in his feud with the State Department.

It is surely not surprising if Europeans concluded that not only was American leadership pointing towards disaster, but that the final debacle, when it came, would be presided over by clowns.

In the United States, however, although many newspapers expressed dismay at the diplomatic clodpollery of Mr. McCarthy's agents, they did not voice the alarm that was felt in Europe. They, too — with notable exceptions — were under the spell of the American fantasy: a fantasy which includes not only the illusion of American omnipotence but also the astonishing assumption that the affairs of other countries, even when their magnitude is that of the Chinese revolution, are primarily " a problem in American politics."

This fantasy must be dispelled and the shocking nature of the truth released in its full impact. The persecution of Americans by other Americans has been substituted for what should be the real aims of American diplomacy. The foreign service of the United States has been largely demoralized. Persecution is depriving the nation of able and effective public servants precisely when their services are crucially important to their country's interest.

It is vital that the American people come to see the difference between incompetence and the inability of public servants to achieve the impossible; American omnipotence is a very dangerous notion and must give way to realism. If they have the confidence of the American people behind them, public servants, free from intimidation, can work effectively on the difficult problems that American leadership, in a world of Communist aggression, must undertake. If they do not have this confidence, they will be ineffectual and our leadership will fail. It is as impossible for a public servant to do his work well under the threat of persecution as it is for a poet to write a sonnet with a gun at his head. And the importance of his work being well done is a matter of consequence, not merely to himself but to all the American people.

It is also vital that the American people reject the assumption that has been foisted upon them that when things go wrong in the world, the cause is American treason. The possibility of actual treason must, of course, keep us constantly alert. But we must refuse to be taken in by the suggestion that because a public official is not submissive to politicians who have set themselves up as the official and sole definers of anti-Communism, he is therefore pro-Communist and a traitor.

There is no room whatever in the present dangerous world for illusion and fantasy. Those who will not face reality eventually collide with it, and the collision is likely to be shattering.

5. The Relentless Reality

It is widely supposed that if the Communists had not frustrated us, we would now be living in a secure and happy world. The truth, unfortunately, is not that simple. The Communists have indeed frustrated us, and the Communist conspiracy is undoubtedly our most pressing problem. Nevertheless, even if Communism did not exist — if, for example, through some immense upheaval, every trace of it were expelled from the Soviet Union and its satellites, leaving Communists in other countries entirely meaningless and without program — the world would still be difficult and dangerous.

Europe, for instance, would be concerned with Germany. What assurance would there be, apart from plans for European unity which at present no one is taking seriously, that Germany would not for a third time involve the world in a disastrous war? The ferment in Asia would also continue. Even though no longer Communist, China would still be revolutionary; and what reason is there for supposing that the Chinese leaders would look to the West? New movements, different from Communism but just as menacing, might very well emerge — as fascism did, and then Nazism, in the aftermath of the First World War. India, too, would be problematical; and the Middle East and Africa.

The point is that history has reached a critical juncture

quite apart from the Communist challenge. The world is now, no matter how reluctantly, a single but disorderly community. It possesses, and will continue to possess, extremely dangerous weapons. If it remains disorderly, even though Communism should vanish, other contenders would arise; before long the equivalent of our present antagonisms would have emerged, and once more, civilization would be faced with mortal peril.

The fact is, of course, that Communism *does* exist and shows no sign of vanishing, but the value of seeing our situation as though Communism had no part in it is that it draws our attention to the wider problems which must be solved. Before there can be security, the entire world must be organized on a basis that will satisfy not only the Western nations but all mankind. Until it is, there will be ferment and unrest. There is thus no possibility, even apart from Communism, of the United States returning to its former, less demanding place in the world. Americans, therefore, instead of resenting the new conditions and allowing themselves to be provoked into persecutions, scapegoat-hunting, and strife between themselves, should adjust themselves to the realities: realities which nothing can dissolve and which, no matter what we wish, remain inexorable and relentless.

Nor can it ever be enough, in facing these realities, to think only in terms of their external form, as though they were problems in mechanics. They are moral problems, too, and cannot be solved by political expedients: they must be solved by righteousness.

The American people have partly understood this, and since the end of the war, through UNRRA, the Marshall Plan and other enlightened projects, they have practiced an unparalleled benevolence. It is neither true nor useful to reproach the people of the United States for inadequate moral aims without at the same time recognizing the high moral standards which have prompted many of their recent undertakings. It can even be questioned, without impropriety, whether any other nation since the dawn of history has given so freely of its substance to the needs of the world as the United States has in the last few years. This is our cause for hope. We are capable of high moral purpose.

Nevertheless, we must not leave out of sight the real dimensions of the claims upon us. They are claims not only for generosity with material things, but for an equally generous comprehension of the need to participate fully and unselfishly in making the world a neighborhood. The harshness of a McCarran Act undoes the good of generous material aid.

Equally important are our patience and tolerance, our sympathy and humility — and most of all, our genuine willingness to face the problems of a difficult world. If, under the stress of these problems, we forsake among ourselves the moral standards which have guided us, and the principles bequeathed to us by the Founding Fathers, we shall have lost our most essential asset in the struggle for the triumph of our cause.

The predicament of the modern world, with its burdens and frustrations, can bring out the worst in us if we so choose — or if, by default, we permit it. But it can also bring out the best. We can put an end, if we will, to our reluctance to take a full and generous part in shaping history towards a happier future: a reluctance that is the spawn of malice and mistrust — from the guilt of which unhealthy consciences take refuge in accusing others and thus pave the way for persecution.

The predicament of the modern age will not be ended until our higher morality has triumphed over selfish aims. We are involved in a struggle which is sure to issue either in the greatest advancement of freedom, justice, and benevolence the world has ever known, or in the destruction of the civilized world and the general degradation of mankind. If we are to avert this latter alternative, we must divest ourselves of all the ancient, worn-out, plausible excuses with which we have procrastinated in the past, and become committed, fully and sincerely, to the law of God that makes each of us throughout the world, his brother's keeper. This we must do — not as a matter of affirmation and sentiment, empty of practical effect, as has been the case so often in the past, but through social and political action, replacing evil with good, and turning wrong into right.

If the problems of the present time are to be solved, it must be through patient and unfaltering realism; if dangers are to melt away, it must be through steadfast and enduring courage; if a better world is to be built, it must be upon the basis of our highest moral principles. If we will recognize that these are the claims that history has made upon us and are willing to begin to meet them, the fear and mistrust that are sapping our strength, and the dissensions that are robbing us of unity will all dissolve away and there will be no room for persecution.

As for the greatness of the task, the prayer for courage is the one that never goes unanswered.

PART TWO

THE FRUITS OF FRUSTRATION

6. The Flight from Freedom

The urge to persecute, though always latent, cannot get very far in a country where freedom is loved and human rights respected. The extent, therefore, to which persecution becomes active and is not rebuked by public opinion is also the extent to which freedom is no longer loved and respect for human rights is languishing. What, then, in this respect, is our present situation?

First, let us go back a little. We have rather lightly assumed, at least until recently, that the majority of people desire freedom. The Western world, and particularly the United States, was born from the struggle to be free. There is no way of recalling our history which does not make freedom the ascendant star in the constellation of our national values. Democracy, here or anywhere, is inexplicable without it. Our deepest urge is to be free.

So we say. And we suppose, because no one takes issue with us that there is no dissent; that we are all of one opinion. But we may be mistaken. If we regard Germany as belonging with the Western world, we should remember how short a time it is since that nation — or the greater part of it — willingly renounced freedom and surrendered to the authority of Hitler. This was not merely a political concession, inspired by nationalist ambition; it was a spiritual affirmation. The authority of Hitler was preferred to freedom. It was scarcely otherwise with Mussolini's Italy.

Since the Second World War, in one country after another, freedom has been relinquished in favor of Communist authority. It is true that these countries were taken over by force; but it is also true that before this happened, enough Communists had been elected to form a decisive minority. Is freedom desired, then, as much as we thought — or as much as it used to be? Even in America there are those who are tired of it, and although they are not clearly aware of it or ready as yet to be regimented politically, they are spiritually in search of authority.

Freedom frustrates them. It has brought them no secure convictions, no refuge from confusion, no escape from cross-purpose, no rescue from futility. Since American traditions have shaped their minds, they are attached to freedom's forms but disenchanted with its substance. That is why they feel no anger when inquisitorial committees try to frighten people into accepting fear-ridden standards of conformity. They do not feel within themselves the value of the free-mind principle.

Not that they have turned away from freedom. But they feel that something is wrong and new disciplines are needed to set it right. There must be authority — something defined and clear, something that takes command. If this mood is combined with emotional factors later to be discussed, and if circumstances provide the inducement and the opportunity, it may lead to joining the Communist Party. Besides authority and discipline, the Party gives its members definite aims in the service of which they can live purposeful lives, and an overall philosophy which, to those who accept it, interprets the world in ways that are meaningful. There is also the pretense, persuasively presented, that Communist authority, though not compatible

with the waning liberties with which the candidate is disenchanted, prepares the way for a better and more useful
kind of freedom.

A person, however, who joins the Communist Party primarily on the basis of this promise and not because he
wants to join a conspiracy is not likely to remain in it very
long.   Nevertheless, when he leaves it, he will probably
look for some other kind of authority.   He may find it in
a church.   If this is impossible because he cannot believe
what the church teaches, his quest becomes more difficult
and he may be drawn into the new, as yet amorphous movement that is growing up in America: the so-called anti-
Communist crusade that is really a campaign against the
free mind and the traditional American principles.

It is more probable, statistically, that he will join this
" crusade " without ever having been a member of the
Communist Party — indeed, without ever having considered it.   If his intelligence is such that he is repelled by
what he may call the " excesses " of the " crusade," he may
frown upon it and yet wish for some authoritarian disci-
plinc that would discredit the remaining minority who believe in freedom and civil rights.   In this case, he will not
actively support the campaign against those he disdainfully
calls " liberals " (who are being persecuted on the false
charge that because they have shown concern for human
welfare they are pro-Communist); but he will not hinder
it, either.

At this point he may be a little taken aback to discover
that he is in unexpected company.   Not all of those who
are in retreat from freedom are disillusioned with it because
they think it has failed them spiritually.   Many are hostile
to it because it has permitted criticism of anti-social prac-

tices — such as profit-making without regard to human welfare. They would like to silence the free-speaking teachers in schools and colleges who are bold enough to point out evils in the capitalistic system, and who leave their students with the thought that, for the benefit of all concerned, such evils should be remedied.

These are the same people who in the 1920's thought that Mussolini might be on the right track, and in the 1930's that the United States might be none the worse for a little of what Hitler was doing in Germany. In many cases, they held to this attitude even after the Second World War had started: as, for example, the America-Firsters and their satellite groups who were only silenced after Pearl Harbor. At that time, *they* were the " fellow-travellers " who shared the Communist view (until Hitler attacked Russia) that the war was not an American concern but just a struggle between rival European imperialisms.

Even now, after full disclosure of the barbaric evil of the Hitler regime with its militarism, racism, genocide and gas chambers, these people are unwilling to acknowledge the consequences of dealing carelessly with human rights or to recognize as inevitable this outcome of a retreat from freedom. But there *is* an inevitable outcome, and those who are unwilling to foresee it are just as much engulfed in it, sooner or later, as are its earliest and most obvious victims.

The fact is that in the modern world the retreat from freedom is inseparable from calamity. This was proved by the Nazis and the fascists who retreated from it with the approval of capitalists, and has equally been proved by the Communists, from whom capitalists have withheld approval. Just as it is impossible to exchange authority for freedom without a struggle — and often a fierce and bloody one, as history reminds us — so it is impossible to revert from freedom to authority without a catastrophic loss.

This is the first thing that should be understood, both by those who have found freedom spiritually frustrating and those who fear that it may limit profit-making. There is "no way back" from freedom that is not calamitous. Whatever burdens it imposes, whether they be the pain and labor of independent thought or merely the constraint of public opinion upon unbridled greed, must either be borne or exchanged for heavier burdens. Indeed, the metaphor is quite inadequate: in these years of the cold war and the hydrogen bomb, it is not a matter of the comparative weight of burdens, but of whether freedom and reason ensure survival or tyranny and folly involve us in a measureless disaster.

The association of the spiritual frustrations of freedom with the fear of the exposure of economic and social evils which it permits may seem to be rather a wide stretch, and without much attention to categories. The answer is that whether wide or not, it is a stretch that is frequently covered within the bounds of a single personality. A man can feel tired of the freedom that has frustrated him spiritually and at the same time be hostile to the freedom that impedes his self-interest; and the two can be related. If his motivation were higher, he could use his spiritual freedom with less impairment of vision and greater possibility of making his life meaningful, his conscience wholesome, and his activity morally purposeful.

It is not without interest that in modern America the quest for authority began by identifying it with material success. Because Henry Ford had discovered a method for making automobiles more briskly and more numerously than other people had been able to make them, he was accepted as an authority not only on automotive engineering, which would have been appropriate, but also on theology, philosophy, sociology, economics, and most of the subjects in a university curriculum. When, therefore, Mr. Ford solemnly informed his fellow-citizens that " history is bunk," many of them unhesitatingly believed it.[1] This was a pity because history was catching up with America even faster than Ford cars were rolling off the assemblylines, though a lot of people only discovered it when it overtook us in the attack on Pearl Harbor.

In the same way, it was considered important in the 1920's to know what a sensational novelist thought about life after death or whether a popular crooner could testify to an unfaltering belief in the existence of God.

This was certainly no precipitate retreat from rationality, but it did indicate to a sensitive observer both the spiritual emptiness from which the yearning for authority emerged and the uncritical way in which authority was sought and its dicta accepted. How far is it from this to accepting McCarthy as an authority on Communism?

But what *is* authority? What is it that people tired of freedom hope to find? The word itself derives, of course, from the same root as the word *author*, and indicates the power of originating and therefore of controlling what-

---

[1] He himself subsequently modified this opinion. During the trial of his law-suit against the *Chicago Tribune* on July 15, 1919, the cross-examining counsel forced him to admit that his own case rested in part on things that had happened in the past and which were therefore history and asked him whether he still believed that history is bunk. Pressed for an answer, Mr. Ford replied, " I don't say I don't believe in it."

ever it is that is originated. The greatest authority on Euclidian geometry was presumably Euclid, since he originated it. In the case of Freudian psychology, it would be Freud; in the case of theories of relativity, Albert Einstein. In these instances we have no difficulty unless it be the possibility that such originators have been outmarched by pupils or disciples who have improved upon their masters and therefore surpassed them in authority.

The point is, however, that in anything that can be demonstrated, as most things can in science, authority is based upon achievement — achievement, be it noted, that can be tested and proved, and made to stand upon its merits. Such authority is rational: it indicates that on a given subject there are those who know more than is known by other people and whose knowledge is open to inquiry.

But if we are told, for instance, that an opinion is authoritative because it has been held for a long time and by a large number of people, we are up against such facts as that a large number of people believed for many centuries that the sun makes a daily journey around the earth whereas the truth was known only to the very few who had evidence that the earth revolves upon its axis. Similarly, a large number of people believed for a long time that the gods were very numerous and that they lived on Mt. Olympus; and that disease is caused by " humors " that float through the air in the night-time; and that the universe is composed of only four elements, earth, air, fire and water; and that it is impossible for man to fly, since he is not equipped with wings: and a thousand other things that have been believed by multitudes of people for a long-continued period.

There is no authority whatever conferred by longevity

or the weight of mere numbers — unless we arbitrarily impute it. Nor is authority increased when to numbers and age we add unusual dignity. The medical profession is numerous and has existed for a long time and it had unusual dignity in nineteenth century Europe. Yet it insisted that childbed fever was not carried by the doctors from the autopsy room to the hospital ward and thus from one mother to another. Only one man insisted otherwise — the Hungarian physician, Semmelweiss. He was derided, persecuted, hated, scorned — but he was right. The entire medical profession, with its numbers, age, and dignity, was wrong — and continued to be wrong until it listened to the evidence.

So has it been again and again, for century after century. For it is simply not true that because a thing has been believed by a multitude of people, or for a long period, it is therefore authentic. Authority in this sense is merely attributed and exists only for those who are willing to acknowledge it. In other words, *the believers themselves confer the authority out of their own believing.* They seldom stop to notice it, but what they are doing is projecting their own consent into something external, something which has the " right " to command obedience. The proof of it is that when they withdraw their consent, there is nothing there.

That is what those who are tired of freedom must do if they want authority: they themselves must create and validate it by their own surrender. Nor is this changed if a multitude goes with them. The surrender of millions can no more make a thing valid than the surrender of a single individual.

The source of authority in human society is nothing but

the people's consent. And the people are wise, as all history makes plain, if they make their consent conditional and protect it with laws and bills of rights. It must be a limited consent and one which, at any time, they can withdraw. And it must be lighted by the lamp of reason. In short, there is no other way than freedom — no matter how strenuous or how unsheltered the way of freedom may be. That is what the Founding Fathers knew, and what many of their children have forgotten.

What those who are tired of freedom want is therefore not available. There is no institution or agency to which they can trust themselves, and no movement which asks them to surrender their freedom which is not the reflection of their own defeat. There is no external authority — and there cannot be one — which is not their own weakness written large. And out of these deficiencies and their moral emptiness no good can come, whether it be through Communism or a false Americanism.

On the contrary, they will bring disaster. With freedom abdicated and the little light of reason extinguished, there would be no hope whatever, as the world now stands, of saving civilization — and not much, perhaps, even of human survival. In the clash of tyrannies would come the final disaster.

In the past, it may have been otherwise: if freedom was lost, there were degrees of servitude. But now, at history's climax, the flight from freedom is the flight from life. There are no alternatives.

7. What Makes a Communist?

The age at which an American is most likely to become a Communist is apparently between 18 and 23. According to Ernst and Loth, whose study of American Communism is indispensable reading to anyone who prefers facts to the lurid ambiguities of popular assumption, "a majority of the rank and file have not only joined but have left the party by the time they are 23." [2]

Whatever else this may signify, it must mean that becoming a Communist is rather frequently an adolescent revolt against society, perhaps most often against a home presided over by a domineering parent, and Freudians would doubtless relegate it to the more or less normal categories of psychosexual development.

It is also evident that only a very small minority of young people who rebel against society during their transition to adulthood are likely to become Communists. The average number of members in the Communist Party in the United States for the last 23 years is 40,000, or about two-hundredths of one-per-cent of the population.

On the other hand, it is known that, in the United States, about 700,000 men and women have left the Communist Party — which means that far more Americans have ceased to be Communists than have remained such. Since

[2] Morris L. Ernst and David Loth, *Report on the American Communist* (N.Y.: Henry Holt & Co., 1952), p. 2.

it is far from easy to leave the Communist Party, once a person has been in it for any length of time, many of these people, in achieving the necessary fortitude and independence, must be assumed to have undergone considerable personal development.

It is believed, however, that the "hard core" of the party is composed of about 5,000 members, and this group, unlike the rank and file, is not subject to much turnover.

It seems desirable, in view of these statistics, to distinguish rather sharply between what might be called the "transient Communist," to whom Party membership is a passing phase of personal development, and the disciplined and tough-minded Communist who belongs to the "hard core." In what follows it is chiefly the latter who is under consideration. This does not mean, however, that those who were only briefly in the Party were not afflicted in many cases with the same emotional disturbances as those who gave durable allegiance to it; but either the intensity was less or they managed to become better adjusted.

It should be noted, too, that Communism is not the only outlet for those emotionally disturbed in these particular ways. Nazism was such an outlet. So was the Ku Klux Klan. So is the pseudo-patriotism of perfervid anti-Communists. In many cases, where the Communist Party and its organized equivalents are not available — which means in the greater part of the United States — the disturbed personality must express itself through merely local or self-created mechanisms. As, of course, it does, from time to time, when a small town or a rural area becomes afflicted with a "witch-hunting" mania.

One remembers — if a personal note is admissible — that when the newspapers widely report a speech against the excesses of the investigating committees of Congress, the abusive correspondence which comes to one's desk — much of it on postal cards — is strongly symptomatic of this kind of personality distortion. Especially is this the case if one criticizes Senator McCarthy. It is thus evident, as one should expect, that when a persecutor of wide notoriety recruits a following, he attracts to himself many of the emotionally disturbed people who, under other circumstances, might have relieved their tensions by joining the Communist Party.

It is not contended, of course — and this should be emphasized, because in a general analysis there is always great danger of over-simplification — that the motivation of Communists is uniform and unvaried. We must recognize that Communists are people, differing from individual to individual, and subject to all the complexities and vagaries that are found in human nature. Nevertheless, provided we recognize that no analysis can apply to all cases equally, there are facts about Communist motivation which are widely typical.

People do not become Communists because they have been persuaded by Communist doctrine. On the contrary, Communist doctrine persuades them because they have become ready to become Communists. This is not to say that the ideas of Communism are not accepted intellectually or that the Party program is not supported from genuine conviction. The point is that the ideas are accepted and the program supported because the individual concerned is emotionally satisfied by them. If this were not otherwise apparent it would become so as soon as we recall that many of those who join the Party remain in it even when the ideas are distorted and the program plainly compromised. Those who are unable to do this — as was the case with a considerable number at the time of the Hitler-Stalin pact — are denounced by the Party leaders as not being true Communists.

The allegiance of a Communist — an enduring Communist — is not to a system of ideas or to a definite program but to the *Communist conspiracy* against established society, and he is not shaken — not seriously — when the needs of the conspiracy require that doctrine be disregarded and the program perverted and betrayed.

Psychologically, Communism is a religion and the Party the perverse equivalent of a church. It is a religion with a creed, the Communist Manifesto; with a priesthood, the more trusted of the Party members; with a hierarchy, the Communist inner circle; with a messiah, Lenin, and a sepulchre, his tomb; with a holy city, Moscow; with an orthodoxy, whatever the hierarchy decides is such; with a "theology," dialectical materialism; with missionaries, its disciples throughout the world; with an inquisition and a drastic attitude to heretics; with a heaven on earth in the future; with a claim to complete devotion, surpassing that of country or of home — in short, with psychological alternatives to almost everything that other religions offer, and with the emotional satisfactions of a church.

Its appeal, however, is not to the nobler elements in human nature, as the appeal of other religions is, but to resentment and hate. This is sometimes plainly stated, sometimes muffled by the call for justice or hidden behind the parade of comradeship. And the Communist "church" is not an open fellowship but a secret order, disciplined by zealots, and engaged in a conspiracy to rule the world.

In joining the Party, it is not likely that many converts see clearly what they are doing or embrace consciously all that membership implies; yet, they join it because it *is* a conspiracy and releases pent-up rebelliousness and the tensions of frustration; they join it because it satisfies an emotional need.

The same need, as already indicated, was satisfied for many by the Nazi conspiracy with its " fifth columns " conspiring against the existing order. It is not accidental that the behavior of Soviet leaders at conferences and as negotiators is strikingly similar to that of the former Nazi leaders. There is the same truculence, the same denunciatory oratory, the same complaining, the same deliberate adoption of perfidy as a means of getting what you want. The moral basis is never that of genuine participants in the same society, or of sincere negotiators sharing with other negotiators the aim of arriving at a common agreement. The morality and the motivation are those of conspirators — conspirators *against* society and *against* agreements that might benefit society.

If it is argued that Communism is a conspiracy solely against capitalistic society, it is only necessary to recall the name of Tito. He was excommunicated, not for apostasy to Communist principles, or for infidelity to the overall Communist program, but because he was not taking his allotted place in the conspiracy: he was doing too much conspiring on his own.

If we follow this thought a little further, we shall see even more plainly how much it is the key to answering our question. Communists not only conspire against established society, which they intend to overthrow, but they conspire against each other. This is true not only at the level of Stalin against Tito, or Malenkov against Beria: it is true right through the movement. Every Communist functionary conspires continuously against other Communist functionaries. Why? Partly, of course, lest he himself should be conspired against successfully, or lest he seem to lack in zeal. But more than this, because conspiracy is the very stuff of Communism: the motivation that impels it and which it cannot lose.

This is not to say that Communism has no social purposes or that they are never in any degree fulfilled. But whether fulfilled or not, they are the weapons of conspiracy. It is for this reason that the original program of Communism will never be achieved. Communists can never produce the society they promise simply because no society can be better than the people who mold it. Since Communists, to gain power, must become conspirators, and to keep power must remain conspirators, any society they mold and control will be one sown through and through with the spirit and aims of conspiracy.

This is what has happened wherever Communism has come and this is what is still happening. It is therefore indubitably plain that the emotional need that Communism satisfies is the need to conspire. But what are the roots of this need? They are far from obvious. They must be very deeply hidden.

They are indeed. They are as deep as such needs have always been, and they are by no means limited to Communists. Nor are they new. They are as old as the hate of Cain against his brother, Abel. As old as what that legend signifies. When Abel made his sacrifice, the smoke went up to heaven; but in Cain's case, it didn't. Abel, that is to say, was part of a world to which he was adjusted; he got along with it and the gods seemed to smile upon him. But with Cain it was otherwise. So he slew his brother, Abel.

Not that Abel was necessarily an entirely upright man and that there was no justice on Cain's side. Perhaps there was. There is seldom a grudge without some basis for it. Perhaps when Cain began to conspire against Abel, he felt that he had joined a just conspiracy. He was also engaged in the battle of ideas. For Cain was an agriculturist, and part of the significance behind the legend is the idea that civilization, which, of course, was based upon agriculture, was in conflict with the simpler social life that had preceded it.

But we need not concern ourselves with the ideas themselves. The point is that the need Cain felt for killing Abel was not rooted in ideas but in his own inner conflict, his grudge against society. Otherwise, he would have fought the matter out, idea against idea. But, like the Communists, he was not willing to let his ideas take their chance in the open forum. He needed — emotionally needed — to *act*, and drastically. So he exchanged argument for assassination.

It is as old as that. It is as elemental as that. But let us examine it in greater detail. In February, 1950, the newspapers reported the case of Dr. Klaus Fuchs, the London atomic scientist who gave to Soviet agents, over a period of years, complete information on American and British atomic developments. Here was treason at its ugliest — and, by rational standards, its least comprehensible. But rational standards were not the ones to apply: the psychology of treason is a study in the dark hinterland of the emotions.

Dr. Fuchs' father understood this: his explanation was that his son had the mind of a genius and the soul of an infant. He did not mean the soul of an infant in the sense of unspoiled purity or simplicity, but in the sense of arrested spiritual development. The soul of the man was stunted, dwarfed, ungrown. Yet it did not impair his brilliant mentality. This, for many people, is a difficult thing to comprehend, although it occurs quite frequently. There can be a mind like Spengler's, for instance, stupendous, magnificent, but at the disposal of a soul that never grew up.[3] And because it never grew up, it never grew strong enough to bear the burden of a fully human life; and so it became sick and disordered and its sickness contributed to the rise of Hitler and all the malignities of the Nazi epoch of German life.

To a lesser exent, the same may be said of Karl Marx. By a lesser extent, I mean that the sickness of soul was less — not the consequences to the world at large. And so may it be said of Schopenhauer and Nietzsche, and of many another. A brilliant mind cannot of itself unlock the doors of life. Unless the soul can grow — that is to say, the spirituality, the moral discernment, the wide, deep sympathy, the compassion, the inner fortitude which makes it possible to deal strongly with one's own life and gently with other lives: unless this inner mystery of heart and conscience can break forth and go out with a man into the world in which he makes his way — he is forever a weakling and the brilliance of his mind is more likely to ensnare him than to save him.

This is what we can understand when we read the writ-

---

[3] Oswald Spengler, German philosopher and historian, who wrote *The Decline of the West.*

ings of such former Communists as Arthur Koestler. A great many fine-minded people who have never been tempted to treason *could* be tempted to it — if the circumstances of their lives had happened to bring temptation near. They could be tempted because they have not discovered what Koestler did about this inward truth of the human soul.

What is it that happens to an undergrown soul? Let us try to be specific. Let us take such cases as occur — and might occur in greater numbers — in our own American life. The ungrown soul is in revolt against its own frustrations. It hates, perhaps, the neglect or injustice suffered in childhood and sees in every kind of authority that represses or restricts it, the repugnant image of the father. Here, we come to the dark places that modern psychology has been trying to illumine for us. To the oppressions and rivalries of childhood, we can trace many of the feelings of persecution and injury that are carried forward into adult life. Here, also, are the hated inferiorities: inferiorities in attractiveness, in talent, in virility, in any of a hundred ways — inferiorities which the stunted soul refuses to accept as real but attributes instead to the evil nature of the outer world which is constantly insulting and rejecting it. The greater success of others is due to injustice, never to their superior abilities, and so the success of others is hated and resented.

Gradually, a secret malice poisons the soul and prevents its growth. Instead of sympathy going out to others, it is reserved for oneself. Right becomes an expression, partly of a rational desire for justice and partly of this hidden, secret mutiny. Wrong is whatever stands in the way of what the distorted soul is wishing for. Not, of course, that these facts are recognized — except sometimes in the office of a psychiatrist, or through a spiritual liberation or conversion. On the contrary, these evil motives unite themselves with higher ones and turn their victim into a crusader. The higher motives are just as genuine as the evil ones, but the evil ones gain the ascendancy. And thus an individual who is a Communist (or a Nazi: it is the same motivation) partly because he is a reformer who wants to remedy injustice, becomes in the end a conspirator against human society because he hates human society. He hates it because it has not given him what he wanted, and out of this hatred comes such a monster as Hitler and all the lesser Hitlers of the entire Nazi psychosis; out of this hatred, also, comes the malignant inner core of the Communist movement, highly developed mentally and stunted in soul.

Out of the dark depths of this same cavern of human frustration comes the moral surrender that refuses henceforth to discover right and wrong for oneself, but submits instead to an authority, a vengeful authority, an authority that is on the side of the sick soul's maliciousness and which promises to destroy the last vestiges of the spiritual authority which the soul has rejected. The Kremlin is the father-substitute, the god-substitute, the symbol of mutiny enthroned in the sky. And so it becomes two things at once: the focus of the soul's revolt and at the same time the tranquillizer, the blesser and soother of the ill-adjusted individual conscience.

To those who have not seen as much as some of us of the shadowy complexities of human life, the psychology of all this is rather elusive; so let us try to describe it once more, in a rather different way. The soul is childish and undergrown. But the mind is well developed. This means that spiritually and morally the things a child wants are the things the adult Communist wants. He wants to accept authority and to have its approval — this is a powerful psychological urge — and at the same time to avoid being restrained, to rebel violently against authority. He can only achieve this contradiction — or seem to achieve it — by accepting an authority, the Communist hierarchy, which is itself in revolt against all other authority, including the authority of prevailing standards of right and wrong. In this way, it is possible to rebel against the parental image and at the same time be accepted and guided by the parent-substitute. That is the first thing.

The second is that restraints are removed in such a way that inferior people, by becoming conspirators, can cause themselves to feel superior. They belong to an elite — the conspiracy. They can indulge their malice against society. It is not necessary to make a personal effort at adjustment; instead of this the society can be made to adjust to one's own undergrown soul. The hated superiorities which one cannot oneself attain can be dragged down and trampled on — and all in the name of justice and restitution.

Meanwhile, there can be tantrums and name-calling, as witness Hitler or the Soviet delegates at the United Nations — obvious manifestations of arrested emotional development and symptoms of prolonged childhood. The malicious instincts of an undisciplined but precocious child can be combined with plausibly right aims and higher idealisms: right and wrong, so to speak, can both be done at the same time. *Right*, that is to say, as the mind contrives to justify it, *wrong* as it exists in hidden motivation. One can have approval — the approval of the parent-substitute, or the god-substitute — for doing *wrong*; and at the same time pretend that wrong is done only that *right* may eventually prevail.

This is the sickness of the stunted soul that makes it easy for apparently honorable men to turn to treason. In some such men, the sickness of soul is less and the idealism more, especially at the beginning. In others there is almost no idealism whatever; nothing but sickness of soul. And the worst of it is that highly intellectual types — types, also, which are emotionally sensitive — are very susceptible to this spiritual underdevelopment. And so minds grow strong only to get lost. And souls are too weak, and after a while too sick, to help the minds to find their way.

But by no means must we suppose that it is a malady that expresses itself only in fascism and Communism and revolutionary movements. The virulence varies, but in one degree or another it is the underlying cause of almost all that goes wrong in human affairs from the level of the United Nations to that of the home and the individual.

Unfortunately, it is too seldom brought out into the day-light and sufficiently understood. Even religion, at its usual levels, seldom really grapples with it. Religion, of course, does emphasize — and it is a very important empha-sis — that we must develop an outgoing love and learn the meaning of brotherhood: and it is true that we must. And when religion tells us to love our neighbors as ourselves, the command on the face of it is good. But when we come to look into it we are struck with a shocking sense of irony. Our trouble is that we *do* love our neighbors as ourselves — we feel towards them, that is, just about what we feel for ourselves. For the truth is that many of us do *not* love ourselves; we *hate* ourselves.

Sometimes, we hate them so much that we are entirely

unwilling to look at them — to see ourselves as we are.   But deep within the subtleties of our souls, we *do* know our- selves as we really are.   And what we know, we hate.   Then, because it is intolerable to admit to such a self-hatred, we transfer it from ourselves to other people.   We form a fantasy, a very comforting fantasy, of what we are *really* like, or would be if only we had the chance that other peo- ple have.   We tell ourselves that these other people repre- sent an injustice done to ourselves and we become conspira- tors against them.

This impulse, as we have seen, can express itself aggres- sively through our joining — or favoring — revolutionary movements; it can make us Communists.   It can also make us other things, almost if not quite as bad: persecutors, for instance, of our fellow-citizens against whom we bring false accusations; or applauders of such persecutors.

But however it expresses itself, the impulse becomes, as we have already said, the chief cause of maladjustment in all things human from the quarrels of nations to the unhappi- ness of homes.   It is in the home, of course, that it usually begins.[4]   And sometimes parents greatly contribute to it. This is one of the most important discoveries of modern psychology, but we have not yet succeeded in making suffi- cient use of it.   Too many parents, themselves emotionally impaired, dominate their children, or warp their develop- ment through rejection or favoritism, or infect them with their own frustration feelings and hostilities, or take flight from the home in various " causes."   And so the children of some of them become Communists.

---

[4] See Ernst and Loth, *op. cit.*, Chapter 4.

To defeat Communism, we need new and deeper insights, the first of which is that the evils of society are rooted, not in impersonal factors but in people, and that the hatreds that afflict the world begin with hatreds that are hidden within the dark recesses of individual souls.

8. And Other Persecutors

Every normal human infant — so the psychologists tell us — passes through what is called the " omnipotent stage." He expects all his wishes to be gratified, his moods humored, and his behavior approved. Whatever frustrates him provokes his wrath. Regarding himself as the center of the universe, or at least of all the universe of which he is aware, he seeks compliance. Everyone and everything must always say " Yes." The word " No " he cannot abide.

If he is fortunate, he will leave this stage in due time and learn to accommodate himself to realities. He will accept the fact that dominance is denied him, that a great deal of the world is not concerned about him, that he can have only a little of what he wants, and that even this little is precarious. Instead of approbation and concurrence, he will expect opposition and divergence. And so, besides the word " yes," which he likes to hear, he will adjust himself to the word " no," and not be too put out about it. In other words, he will have forsaken the childish stage, with its illusion of omnipotence, for the more adult stage, leading towards emotional maturity. But, as I say, this is something that only happens if he is fortunate.

If his development is arrested, which it may be if he is over-indulged — or, as we say, " spoiled " — and which it also may be if he is too much thwarted so that he develops the habit of antagonism — he remains emotionally a child.

This need not mean that his intellectual powers are limited. Unhappily, as we have already noted, it is possible to develop a quite considerable intellect and still remain emotionally an infant. Or — and of course this is what most frequently happens — it is possible to live an adult life as something more than an emotional infant and yet without becoming emotionally grown up. In this event, there is a *certain amount* of adjustment to a world that frequently says "No," but a concealed determination to resist that world as much and as often as possible.

Now, if it happens that the adjustment is great enough and the personality as a whole healthy enough, this resolve to change the world can be a useful thing. Guided by intelligence and restrained by forbearance, it seeks its ends through influence and persuasion. Its aim is to convince, to change opinions, to convert others to one's own beliefs and purposes. But if the adjustment is insufficient, or the personality as a whole not healthy, the hidden resolve becomes an urge to dominate. If the world cannot be changed by persuasion, recourse must be had to coercion. Other people *must* believe, *must* conform; they *must* be made to accept and endorse whatever is resolved upon. Otherwise, they challenge and frustrate one's wish for dominance, they stand in the way of a world that answers to one's wishes, they undermine one's confidence. Therefore, they must be roughly dealt with, harassed, repressed — persecuted! Until they are either driven to conformity, or, if they refuse, eliminated.

And thus arises the urge to persecute. Strong minds and strong wills are at the service of childish emotions. Nothing will do that does not reflect one's own image in other people, ratifying one's own beliefs, approving one's own

wishes, confirming one's own purposes. The world must
be the child's world, in which the unadjusted ego is omnipotent, or tries to be; but with this difference: in the emotionally arrested adult, omnipotence keeps company with
omniscience. Not only must one's will prevail but one's
opinions, too. They are "correct" opinions. All others
are false. There is thus a craving not only for compliance
with one's purposes but also for conformity with one's
views. As well as being the unerring arbiter of right and
wrong, one has now become the infallible judge of true and
false. And since to an adult mind, even though its motivation may be childish, this is a difficult position to maintain,
an attempt is made to reinforce it by identification with
external sanctions.

The boldest and yet one of the commonest cases is that
in which the ego projects itself into the ultimate mysteries
of the universe and calls its own projection God, who thereupon is brought in as an unassailable authority. The omnipotent ego is now completely fortified; opposition is sacri-
lege, disbelief is blasphemy; for it has united itself with its
own projection and this projection must be obeyed as God.

Persecution is now much easier. It is not oneself the
heretic is challenging; the challenge is directed against the
Deity. And so emerges religious persecution. It is *right*
to oppress the heretic, for the heretic is not only frustrating
one's own will to dominance: he is rebelling against God.

Or, if we wish to see the same phenomenon with God
left out of it — and psychologically, it *is* the same phenomenon — one's own will is projected as that of "The
People" interpreted inerrantly by their dictator, or of Mani-
fest Destiny, or Historical Determinism, or of any other
substitute, equally mystical, equally hallucinatory, standing

in the place of the self-projected God. For, let it be noticed, when it is the " Will of the People " that is being venerated, every possible precaution is taken against the people being consulted. Both the dictator himself and those who are mystically identified with him are in fact antagonistic to the people's will except where it coincides with their own; they have assumed its authority by displacing it at the same time that they are asserting it. The same is true when the authority of God is invoked for religious persecution; no difficulty is admitted in discovering what the will of God may be: psychologically, the question is irrelevant since the will of God has been displaced by the will of the persecutors who have asserted it.

Or we might take an example from nearer home. An ambitious American politician with a not very gifted mind but an ample supply of craftiness is not making the rapid progress that he thinks he should. The country is largely unaware of him. Unsuited in mentality and character to creative statesmanship and too hungry for power to accept the minor role allotted to him, he knows that what he wants can only come to him through demagoguery. For this he is well equipped, and Communism provides him with his opportunity.

By exploiting the people's fears and exciting their suspicion and mistrust, he misleads considerable numbers of them into thinking that he is their foremost champion in the struggle against the Communist conspiracy. He identifies his own will with the will of the people to defeat Communism and thus convinces many of them that whatever opposes the will of this one man is by necessity pro-Communist. His own aims, personal and political, are sanctioned by the cause he has " taken over "; whatever he does, no matter how unscrupulous, is justified by his anti-Communism. Communism is whatever he says it is and a Communist is whomsoever he declares to be such. To disagree with his opinions is heresy; to oppose his will is treason to the anti-Communist cause.

This man's claim, so far as he is able to maintain it, is the same as Hitler's; his position in the minds of his followers is what Stalin's was for Communists. His own wishes are projected into the anti-Communist cause and are given its sanction and authority. The wishes of his followers, identified with that of their supposed champion, are similarly disguised and dignified. Anti-Communism now has its orthodoxy, which it will enforce upon all within reach of it, and its high priest, who will wield its authority. Thus, in America as in Germany or Russia, conformity is exacted and the situation is ripe for persecution.

Let us return, however, to our analysis of motivation. Down to now, we have thought of the urge to persecute as though it came only from this one source — the craving for omnipotence, the desire to make the world conform to one's own wishes. For the most part, this is indeed the source. Perhaps, in the broad sense and fully interpreted, it is the only source. But if so, it has other emphases. There are those, for instance, who give up the wish to dominate because they are deficient in personal force and not capable of it. In this event, they welcome and support the persecutions led by others, less because they need to feel confirmed in their omnipotence (though the wish is not absent) than because they want to be consoled for their inferiority. They can be happy only if there is nothing better than themselves. They are represented by the famous though anonymous citizen of Athens who was encountered on election day by Aristides the Just. He did not recognize Aristides and it therefore seemed to the latter a good opportunity to find out which way things were going. " Are you voting for Aristides ? " he asked. " No," the citizen replied. " Why not? " asked Aristides. " Has he not given you honest government? " " Yes," the citizen replied, " I suppose he has. But I am tired of hearing him called ' the Just.' "

There is also in the urge to persecute a considerable element of fear. If there are people who do not believe as you do, it becomes harder to suppress your own doubts. If you believe in the superiority of the white race, for instance, and you meet a man who doesn't, it becomes a little less certain that your belief is well founded. Here is a man with a mind, an intellect, similar to your own, and he has come to a different conclusion. Your own conclusion is therefore to that extent unsettled. Here, also, is a man who has dismissed the possibility of something which, presumably, he would like to have believed in. It is therefore conceivable that he has outgrown you emotionally. This is an unpleasant thought. Moreover, his opinion, as over against yours, sounds morally superior. You do not like this man. He threatens your confidence in your own opinions. If he is a respected man, a man of high intelligence, you dislike him that much the more — and you do so because his intelligence intensifies the threat. You are made to reflect that your own intelligence is probably less high. So you must oppose this man or he will weaken your opinions. He is offensive to your self-respect. He is a reproach to you.

Thus reflecting, you become ready to persecute him. You no longer argue with his views; you call him names. You tell yourself and your neighbor that since this man does not conform to prevailing opinion on racial superiority,

very likely he has other " radical " opinions. The use of the
word " radical " brings you much comfort; also a suggestion,
a very pleasing insinuation: since he is " radical," he may be
a Communist. But why " may be "? He *must* be: an un-
doubted threat to society, wicked, immoral. And so, out of
fear, as well as from your other motives, you feel the urge
to persecute.

Sometimes, these persecution sources all flow together.
Within a single mob you will have the domineering type of
persecutor, the frightened type which I have just described,
and also the type that persecutes from a feeling of inferiority. (All these emotions can also vacillate within the same
individual, of course, but one of them will usually rise to the
top and become mainly characteristic.) If enough people
come together under the pressure of excitement, and if they
are manipulated by skillful demagogues who inflame their
passions, the result is a malignant fever, and we have race
riots, religious persecutions, political purges, witch-hunts,
pogroms and the like.

No longer can we suppose that these things belong to the
past or that if they have recurred in other places, they
could never do so in America. We have recently seen the
persecution of public officials, government workers, and
prominent private citizens in alarming numbers and for
reasons no more substantial than those of the witch-hunts
of the seventeenth century.

Nor must we argue that the comparison is unjustified
because Communists are real whereas witches did not exist
except in the imagination of fanatics. Witches *did* exist.
Whether they could do the things attributed to them is another matter, but there is no doubt whatever that some of
them thought they could. There were well organized or-

ders of witches in both England and France, and the heads of the orders were sometimes members of the nobility. Whether there were witches in Salem is another question to which, very likely, no one knows the answer. Even these actual witches, of course, did not deserve the fate meted out to them — not usually, at any rate. But the point is — the point of greatest importance in making the comparison — that hundreds of women who were *not* witches were killed. Sometimes they were killed just because they were more beautiful than other women thought they should be; or because they gave too much evidence of vitality. Or because someone had a grudge to settle. Many times the trials were utter mockeries of justice. In some cases, when the execution of a death sentence was by drowning, both the authorities and the populace were content to let the manner of her drowning settle the woman's guilt or innocence. If she floated, she was obviously a witch; if she sank she was innocent. But in either case, she was dead. The fact that if she sank she would be given Christian burial as an innocent person must have been rather frugal solace to the one condemned to die.

It is true that our modern witch-hunters seldom kill their victims, at any rate in the United States and at the time these words were written: they just ruin their lives. And by many people, this is taken lightly: they have not stopped to think what it means to lose one's reputation and one's chance to make a living: or even what it means, to a loyal citizen, to lose faith in his country and its justice. There are even those who rejoice in these evils and are not afraid that they themselves will be caught up in the greater evils which, unless prevented, are the inexorable outcome.

Such people, of course, although they would loudly deny

it, are uncertain in their own loyalty, infirm in their convictions, afraid to practice democracy and unwilling to defend it.

In her dramatic poem, *Conversation at Midnight,* the late Edna St. Vincent Millay, whose true stature her country has not yet fully recognized, wrote these words: " What a man believes, he lives with quietly." She did not mean that he kept his beliefs a secret, that he was not willing to utter them, that he had no zeal to advance them. What she meant was that he did not get into a panic when he discovered that there were other people who believed differently. His own confidence was not undermined because there were those who did not share his convictions. He had no urge to persecute. On the contrary, he expected to win through persuasion. He was devoted to free and open inquiry. He thought that truth would prevail through its own intrinsic superiority if it were given sufficient opportunity. It was in this sense that what he believed, " he lived with quietly."

Nor did she imply that he would not fight for the right of truth to be freely debated. She did not mean in the least that he was unconcerned at a threat to liberty, or not ready to fight — and even die, if need be — for what he counted finally important. All she meant was that he was confident enough, secure enough in his own faith, his own purposes, to have no fear that they could be taken away from him. He felt no temptation to shout down other people, no impulse to abuse his neighbor for his differing opinions — and no urge to persecute.

It is not easy to maintain that level in these difficult and dangerous days. But it *has* been maintained in days just as difficult and almost as dangerous. The Founding Fathers, for instance, maintained it. So did Lincoln. And it was he who said, "Let us readopt the Declaration of Independence, and with it the practices and policies which harmonize with it."

9. The Cult of Mediocrity

There is one category of persecution, particularly in the United States, that is too often overlooked. We allow ourselves to suppose that the only persecutors who do real damage are those in prominent positions, and that their followers and applauders are mostly good people who have been misled. This, unfortunately, is not the case. The urge to persecute is not an unusual malady which afflicts only the vicious few; it is to be found in people who in many ways are wholesome and who form a large proportion of the population.

The fact is — and we must never lose sight of it — that there is good and bad in all of us and the inner conflict between them never ceases. That is why, especially under stress, the persecuting impulse comes out in people who, if they plainly saw what they were doing, would be appalled by it. And in nothing is this more the case than in the applauding of levellers and detractors. Anyone in public life who possesses or develops superior qualities is suspected and distrusted — and may even be hated. No one more than he is the likely target of persecution.

Again and again, a man of unusual gifts which he is ready to place at the service of his country is haled before a Congressional committee and humiliated. The satisfaction this gives to the Committee members is frequently no greater than the satisfaction that is felt by some of those who read about it in the newspapers. This means, of course — and indeed has already meant to a truly serious extent — that men of stature are less and less willing to enter public service. When, through force of character and favoring circumstances, they do enter it, they must be prepared to spend only a part of their time doing the work for which they were appointed, since the rest of it will be needed for defending themselves against detractors.

That is what happened to James V. Forrestal when he was Secretary of the Navy. He thought that if he could deepen his understanding of men and affairs, and become, as the years went by, a modern example of a philosopher-statesman, judicious, free from partiality, superior to the lower motives, zealous in the public interest, he would increase both his self-respect and the esteem in which his fellowmen would hold him. He found instead that his reward was opprobrium, misrepresentation and ill-repute. This forced him after a while to doubt himself so severely that at last he was unwilling to continue so unsatisfactory a life and decided to end it.

Mr. Forrestal had not always sought wisdom. At first, he sought wealth and succeeded in amassing it. From wealth he turned to power, and this also was given him. But neither wealth nor power seemed to him a satisfying aim, even to one able to achieve such aims. And so he sought wisdom. How could he be wise enough, persuasive enough, and firm but gentle enough, to get the right policies adopted and the right provisions made while there was still time? He had also suffered an intimate loss which impelled him to substitute devotion to the public service for the forlorn hope of personal happiness. He wanted to be worthy of respect. He did not seek applause. Just a fair estimate of his value. But instead, he was slandered and rejected. Finally, he broke under the strain of it. And if he died by his own hand, it was because he had first of all been inwardly destroyed by his fellow-citizens.

It is not necessary to claim that Mr. Forrestal was a great man — although he might have become one. It is not necessary to contend that he should have remained in the office that he held — though his services need not have been wasted. He doubtless made mistakes — as any man would who carried his burdens and faced his problems. But none of this is to the point. The point is that he was a superior public servant with unusual ability and unusual devotion. Yet, his enemies found it easy to make him out a sinister person. And there were many who did not know him, had never met him, and had no way at all of evaluating him who gladly adopted this baseless estimate. It was the urge to persecute — to draw down to a sordid level the superior man whom mediocrity resented.

The same kind of obstruction and abuse was the lot of David Lilienthal. His appointment to the chairmanship of the Atomic Energy Commission was hindered and impeded in all possible ways and was confirmed in the end only because of the firm support of Senator Vandenburg — who was himself an outstanding example of the way a man in public life can outgrow the commonplace and advance towards exceptional maturity. But, although his work was of the highest importance to the security of his country, scarcely for a day was Mr. Lilienthal left to attend to it in peace. He was persecuted by Congressional committees until the point was reached — one must assume — when he had to conclude that it was better to resign. Someone else — he must have hoped — might be given a less hampered opportunity. But no one who knew anything about him and was not blinded by prejudice could dispute his superior ability or the completeness of his devotion to the public interest.[5]

In this case as in that of Mr. Forrestal, the active persecution by the relatively few was applauded by the many who find satisfaction in humbling and destroying superiority — even though it be superior devotion to the public interest.

This, undoubtedly, is the most dangerous temptation to which people in the mass can be subjected. Once again, the outstanding example is Hitler's Germany. Hitler represented other things as well as mediocrity — frustration, embitterment and the urge to dominate — but the malignant satisfaction that the multitude took in his mockery of the civilized aspirations of other nations and their leaders was very largely the satisfaction of those who want to drag down whatever is superior to themselves. He, himself, apart from the powerful drive of his malice, was a mediocre man, physically devitalized, emotionally inadequate. Yet out of his own hate and resentment he had drawn forth a demagogic power which enabled him to evoke in the multitude the same perverse passions that had blackened his own soul.

What Hitler could not possess for himself, he was determined to destroy in those who did possess it. By appealing, at a paranoiac moment in German history, to the same impulse in the multitude that he felt in himself, he was

[5] The writer was chairman of a committee that mustered national support for Mr. Lilienthal's appointment and writes from personal knowledge. Not only was the open opposition to the appointment unworthy, but a whispering campaign which accompanied it was altogether sordid.

able to lead it, first into obsession, and then to self-destruction.

Repeatedly, sober thinkers in the United States have warned us that the cult of mediocrity might prove our undoing. President Conant of Harvard University wrote of it in the *Atlantic Monthly*, in May, 1940. But his article aroused a storm of criticism. Mr. Walter Lippmann has frequently referred to it, pointing out that if we insist upon bringing everything down to the dead level of the average, the ultimate result will be disastrous.

He was not expressing a new opinion. It is as old as Plato. Indeed, Plato knew, and from experience, that persecution by the mass can be just as cruel as oppression by a despot. He knew that Socrates was martyred, not primarily because his enemies had deliberately decreed it, but because mass resentment had been stirred up by the demagogues. Seneca, too, felt compelled to say that democracy can be more cruel than wars or tyrants. But what he had in mind was not democracy as a just system of government or as a political expression of human brotherhood, but democracy as an exaggerated equalitarianism, democracy that was trying to base itself upon the lowest common denominator of mass instinct instead of upon the greatest common multiple of democratic aspiration.

A particularly clear admission of the extent to which the demagogue relies upon this motivation in the multitude is made by Harold Lord Varney in a recent article called " The Truth about Joe McCarthy." [6] When we search for the source of McCarthy's popularity, he tells us, we find it " in the legend which is growing up about his name as an un-

---

[6] In the *American Mercury*, September, 1953.

hesitating challenger of the great. The public always reacts tribally to Jack the Giant Killer." (The reader will not fail to note the word "tribally.") Washington, at present, Mr. Varney continues, is a "dismal swamp" of the discredited. McCarthy's targets have all fallen; they were "the men whom others cultivated"; all are now gone but McCarthy is "still there." And he closes his report with this significant sentence: "The little people everywhere have loved the performance."

Mr. Varney's illustration — the hearing at which McCarthy compelled High Commissioner James C. Conant to appear before him — is also not without interest. Dr. Conant, he tells us, is "one of the reigning deities of the American intelligentsia — the venerated spokesman of the whole powerful internationalist clan." It is easy to imagine the satisfaction of Mr. McCarthy, to whom the multitude "reacts tribally," at being able to browbeat a man who possesses one of the finest minds in America, and who has long been known for his integrity, his probity, and his deep devotion to the public interest. But what Mr. McCarthy felt is very secondary; the important and ominous thing is the degree of truth in Mr. Varney's assertion that "the little people everywhere have loved the performance."

When shall we learn that equality does not mean the levelling down of talent, which is impossible, or of personal qualities and character, which is wicked even to desire? As Emerson put it, and not, it would seem, with unnecessary emphasis: "Men of aim must lead the aimless, men of invention lead the uninventive. . . . Whilst the rights of all as persons are equal, their rights in other directions are very unequal. Neither the caucus, nor the newspaper, nor the Congress, nor the mob, nor the guillotine, nor the fire, nor all together, can avail to outlaw, cut out, burn or destroy the offense of superiority in persons."

When we reflect upon the matter rationally, we know that we expect from our public servants both ability and devotion. If they out-perform the common standard, however, emotional impulse takes control, and instead of being grateful for what is obviously to our advantage, we deride it. If this habit of detraction proceeds from equalitarianism, then it is clear that equalitarianism will bring about its own undoing, for a society based upon equality is more in need of able leaders than any other form of society whatever. Mediocre leadership might maintain a feudalism or a tyranny, at least for a while, but not a democracy. Its problems are too difficult.

But then, this view of equality is wrong. That which is better must be acknowledged to be better, and true equality is the equal right of all to be the best they can. As Lincoln put it, saying in another way what Emerson said, " The authors of the Declaration of Independence intended to include *all* men, but they did not intend to declare all men equal *in all respects*."

People had been pestering Lincoln, seeking to discover the extent to which he endorsed the popular idea of equality. He knew perfectly well, he said, that the declaration that " all men are created equal " was the foundational principle of the American Republic; it was a principle that he, least of any, was likely to dispute. He held it as a basic conviction.

But Lincoln also knew that the men who founded the Republic were by no means average men. Was Washington average? Or Jefferson — the very man who wrote the famous Declaration? Were these men not head-and-shoulders above others? Would there have been a Constitution, a Federal Union, a Republic, if average men had faced the situation instead of such men as these?

And so, finally, Lincoln gave his answer. Men were not equal in all respects. They were certainly not equal in " intellect, moral development or social capacity." The Founding Fathers had " defined with tolerable clearness in what respects they *did* consider all men created equal — equal with certain inalienable rights among which are life, liberty and the pursuit of happiness."

It is a great pity that we do not have, instead of the thoughtless worship of the legendary Lincoln, an intelligent appreciation of the true quality of his comprehension. Unswervingly democratic in basic conviction, he was never shallow enough to become a mere leveller. Unerringly, he puts his finger on the vital distinction — all men, he says, are *not* equal in social capacity and moral development: just as all are not equal in physical characteristics. Some are stronger, others weaker. In the same way, some are wiser, others more in need of guidance. If this means anything, it means that some are better fitted to lead, to guide, to govern. They are this by inherent capacity, but also this by moral development.

There is no notion of a permanent *class* of people thus endowed. There is no exclusiveness whatever. The equal right of all is the right of each, to the full extent of his capacity, to go as far as he can in the service of his fellow-men. Superior ability and superior devotion — they must go together — can come from the humblest dwelling in the country just as readily as from the mansion. The so-called " intellectuals " who are frequently derided and persecuted are not a caste set apart. It has been proved again and again that, in America, a good mind, no matter what the environment in which it emerges, can carry its possessor to fame and eminence. This, and not levelling down, is true democracy.

When the demagogue appeals to the mass to deride and destroy those who are best fitted to lead them, he is depriving the populace of its democratic right to be led by the best leaders the democratic process can produce. And he is preparing the way for his own tyranny. No demagogue from the beginning of time ever appealed to the persecuting instinct of the herd for any other reason than that he hoped to ride to power by blunting the perceptions and debasing the moral standards of those he intended to debauch.

Lincoln understood this and, himself a man of the people, placed his own appeal on the solid ground of sound argument and reason. However, the urge to persecute is heedless of logic. And unhappily, as we have said, it is just as bad in a multitude as in a despot. Essentially, it is the evil of envy, the fear of being surpassed. As Francis Bacon wrote as long ago as 1625, " He that cannot mend his own case will do what he can to impair another's." Or as Montaigne wrote, half a century earlier, " Those who cannot attain to greatness avenge themselves by railing at it." But there is a German proverb which tells us where it all ends up. " Envy," it says, " is the sorrow of fools."

Certainly, this dark and unacknowledged envy that urges us to persecute our leaders and revile those who place superior talent at our service could bring us to grief. Added to the persecution conducted in the name of anti-Communism, it could deprive us of the very men we need to lead us through the dangers that will otherwise engulf and overwhelm us. It is true that the inferior is often more comprehensible and reassuring, and that energetic littleness can give to mediocrity the feeling of being represented without being surpassed. It is true that there is something comfortable about the word "regular." We have a special fondness for that word. We mean by it that capable people must be careful to act like ordinary people, and that those in positions of trust must make it clear that they are no better than anybody else. Yet, if they are no better than anybody else, why should they be given positions of trust?

As illustrated in the introduction to this book, men of ability are leaving government service; other men of ability, in many cases, are refusing to enter it. Why should one seek a position in which, sooner or later, he is likely to be humiliated? Why should one lose his peace of mind, his reputation, and the friendliness that sweetens life about him to endure slander and revilement in the service of his country?

The answer is, of course, that one *should*, no matter what the cost. Not merely ordinary patriotism but the urgency of the times requires it. But it takes a courage that not everyone can muster.

It must be the people themselves who bring about a change. Instead of rejoicing in the falsifications and detractions of the persecutors, whose hope is to drag all the people down to their own level by appealing to what is meanest and most unworthy in the multitude, the people should cry out against their treason to our cause. But this will not be done — cannot be done — until the people, too, give up the urge to persecute.

Demagogues rely upon the worst in people for support. Good leaders must rely upon the people's goodness. If it fails them, there is no alternative resource.

10. A Study in Tyranny

The time to deal with tyranny is before it becomes established; once entrenched, it maintains itself with ease against those who could have prevented it. This, unfortunately, is the lesson which, again and again, the human race has learned too late. The little courage which it would have taken to stop a would-be tyrant before he had achieved power was more courage than his prospective victims could muster. They wrung their hands, they muttered their dismay to one another, they whispered their fears — but they did not act. They were too afraid.

And so a time came, as in Shakespeare's *Macbeth*, when it was fitting to declaim:

> " Bleed, bleed, poor country!
> Great Tyranny! lay thou thy basis sure,
> For goodness dares not check thee."

Yes, evil ascends unchallenged, not because it is unrecognized as evil but because good people are not brave enough to check it. It is all in those six short words: " For goodness dares not check thee."

That is what has been happening in our own country in the last few years. Not that we are yet ruled by tyranny; we are still a free people who elect our own government. But we are indulging tyrannous elements that operate under the protection of our government. In the eyes of many, what these elements are doing is not alarming; if there is wrong in it, it must be condoned because of the end it serves — or which they think it serves. They do not see that this is how tyranny has always been excused — until too late! No would-be tyrant announces that his aim is power; he is the protector of the people, warning against their enemies, the popular champion of a plausible crusade, a persecuted hero, intrepid and dauntless amid the host of his detractors. Thus he presents himself, and although his character is plainly manifested by his deeds, thus he is accepted — by too many until it is too late.

The pattern of the tyrant in his rise to power has been well delineated by Professor Alan Bullock in his recent book on the life of Hitler.[7] It is an immensely important book, not merely because of the completeness with which it explains the recent past, but because of its pertinency to the possible future. We have regarded Hitler, not altogether incorrectly, as a peculiarly German phenomenon, the product of one particular culture, deviant from the rest of Europe, and occurring at one particular moment in the tragic course of history. As I say, there is validity in this analysis. For several centuries before Hitler, the Germans had regarded Europe more as a field for conquest than as a civilization to be shared. The military role had been exalted, especially in Prussia, and the Pan-Germanic ferment was never far below the surface. Moreover, there is an intensity about things German which does not seem to characterize most other countries, so that whatever is pursued, be it good or bad, is pursued with concentrated energy. I remember that during the war I was struck with the aptness of a certain piece of doggerel, intended — slander-

[7] Alan Bullock, *Hitler, A Study in Tyranny* (N.Y.: Harper, 1952).

ously! — to be descriptive of women, but actually much more descriptive of the German people. I think it goes like this:

" O the gladness of their gladness when they're glad,
  And the sadness of their sadness when they're sad,
  But the gladness of their gladness and the sadness of their
      sadness,
  Are as nothing to their badness when they're bad."

I concede, then, that there was something unique about the German situation, and something uniquely German about the rise of Hitler. But then, what are we to say of other tyrants? There was something unique about Stalin, too, and he could not have become a dictator — one supposes — in any other country than Russia. Nonetheless, I think we should attend not only to the German-ness of Hitler and the Russian-ness of Stalin but also to what they have in common, not only between themselves but with other modern dictators. If we do that, I think we shall find that all assurance falls away; whatever has happened in one place and in one particular way can happen in other places and in other particular ways. No country, no matter what its composition, and no matter what its previous history, is proof against the possibility of tyranny.

Let us take a look at Hitler, not so much as a German but as a man. His childhood was frustrating; he had a harsh father against whom he was mutinous and an indulgent mother without much understanding. He did poorly at school and was rejected by the Vienna Academy of Fine Arts as unfitted to enter such an institution. To Hitler, this was not evidence of his own inferiority but of the stupidity of the scholastic system. He might have felt the same if he had grown up in Chicago or New York. Presently, he was penniless, an inmate of a large semi-charitable boarding house for men. There he might have been seen from time to time, sitting in a ragged pair of trousers waiting for his clothes to be de-loused. The man sitting on the next bed was his partner, his associate in carpet-beating, and his ally in peddling show-cards, painted by Hitler for the owners of small stores.

To this man, and to any others who would gather about him, Hitler would declare with fiery impetuosity that their misfortune was not due to anything that was wrong with the Austro-Hungarian empire — anything economic or so-ciological — but only to the frustration of the German-speaking peoples, which frustration had been brought about by the Jews. Already, he was turning away from the sordid reality of his own life, with its laziness, rebelliousness, and resentment of social usage and restraints, to a fantasy in which he was identified with the right of Germans to su-premacy. The Jews, because they were attached to a wider culture and appeared to be successful, were the enemies of the German claim to dominance and were succeeding be-cause they were playing the game according to other than German rules. As early as this, Hitler was saying that " it is not by the principles of humanity that man lives or is able to preserve himself above the animal world, but solely by means of the most brutal struggle."

" This," says Professor Bullock, " is the natural philosophy of the dosshouse. In this struggle," he continues, " any trick or ruse, however unscrupulous; the use of any weapon or opportunity, however treacherous, are permissible. . . . Astuteness; the ability to lie, twist, cheat and flatter; the elimination of sentimentality or loyalty in favor of ruthless-

ness; these were the qualities which enabled men to rise;
above all, strength of will. Such were the principles which
Hitler drew from his years in Vienna. Hitler never trusted
anyone; he never committed himself to anyone, never admitted any loyalty. His lack of scruple later took by surprise even those who prided themselves on their unscrupulousness. He learned to lie with conviction and dissemble
with candor. To the end he refused to admit defeat and
still held to the belief that by the power of will alone he
could transform events."

Now, the things to notice in this portrait are not those
which may have been peculiar to the life of a down-at-heels
petit bourgeois in Vienna at the turn of the century.
What we should see is the lack of scruple, the ruthlessness,
the proficiency in lying with conviction — and beneath it
all the hunger for power and the craving for revenge against
a society which refused preferment to a man who had committed himself to brutal struggle in the hope of effacing
his sense of inferiority. Such a man is not necessarily a
product of Vienna; he could emerge in Paris or London
or Baltimore or Philadelphia. He could even, with appropriate adaptations, achieve the same ambitions in an American rural area.

Not until the First World War did Hitler become em-
ployable. As a soldier he was completely happy, sure that
Germany would come at last to victory. His embitterment at German defeat is one of the features of his situation that affords no basis for comparison. But it is not
a necessary feature in the making of a tyrant. Lenin was
not much concerned over the defeat of Russia in 1917,
nor was Stalin. Mussolini arose in an Italy that had shared
the allied victory. Franco became dictator by resisting,

in the interest of reactionary elements, the groping of the
Spanish people towards democracy. Opportunity varies
from case to case, but the opportunism with which opportunity is seized remains a constant. It is characteristic of all
would-be tyrants.

In Munich, in the aftermath of war, Hitler was soon active in political parties which were conspiring against the
Weimar constitution and the national democratic government. By the growing power of his demagoguery and
the unscrupulousness of his treachery, he soon gained control of one of these parties, and led the famous *putsch* in
1923. And here we come to something to notice. The
Bavarian Government, because it shared Hitler's views
about the Weimar constitution, and the influential army
officers, because they shared his hatred of democracy and
believed in the Pan-Germanic purpose he espoused, permitted him to engage in illegal activities. They despised
him but they thought that he was useful. Even his trial,
after the Munich *putsch*, they allowed him to turn into
an occasion for national propaganda, thus giving him a
wide audience and increasing his following. They did not
quite *intend* to do these things — and they did not like
Hitler. But they *did* do these things — in spite of not liking Hitler. His imprisonment was a farce. In actual fact,
he remained the leader of his movement in frequent conference with his deputies. There were features of all this
peculiar to this one particular situation. But there were
features not so limited. The law was flaunted. Fairly decent people, because they thought it served their ends, in-
dulged Hitler, illegally, in what they knew were wrongful
practices; they were careless as to who got hurt and whether
it was just, or who was slandered, or what the lies that

Hitler told. They thought it served an overriding purpose.

They were insensitive to the fact that the law cannot be lightly treated without evil consequences. As William Pitt had long since put it, "Where law ends, tyranny begins." And it might be put more strongly still: "Where law is not enforced, tyranny begins." We can say, I think, that if there be men in any country who are unscrupulous, tyrannical and hungry for power, and if the Government has a case against these men and refuses to press it, so that the law is brought into contempt and the power of these men increased, there is need to be alarmed.[8] Where law is not enforced, tyranny begins. Presently, it entrenches itself. Then, some day, the people wake up, but it is too late. Only at a calamitous cost, if at all, can they regain their freedom.

The German generals discovered — too late — that they were Hitler's captives. They were against his starting the war but could not prevent him; once started, the war seemed justified because of his brilliant victories. So they were even more his captives. They remained such when the war began to go against them. They tried to kill him. But even in that, they failed. Tyranny entrenched is not easily uprooted.

The politicians also discovered — too late — that they were Hitler's captives. First, von Schleicher and von Papen, then all of them, even some of his own collaborators, like Roehm, whom he slew in the famous purge. Not one of them could stand up against him.

The people too, became his captives. They acclaimed him for his victories without war, his triumphs through

---

[8] See Report of the Senate Subcommittee on Privileges and Elections to the Committee on Rules and Administration, "Investigations of Senators Joseph R. McCarthy and William Benton, pursuant to S. Res. 187 and S. Res. 304" (1952).

bullying. They rejoiced in his destruction of Czechoslovakia, his annexation of Austria. But when they knew he
was going to attack Poland, they stood silent in the streets
while the armored regiments drove by. Hitler, looking out
at them from his chancery window was angry and contemptuous. They did not want war. Hitler knew it. The
generals did not want war. Hitler knew that, too. The
politicians were afraid of war. Hitler was aware of it. But
they all did his bidding. They were his captives. For such
is the nature of tyranny.

The Italians, too, were against war. Especially, they did
not wish to be allies of Germany. But Mussolini, like
Hitler, could enforce his will and did enforce it. So Europe
was devastated and Hitler's Germany lay in ruins. Such is
the evil spawned by tyranny.

Of course, in the end, evil brings about its own undoing.
It is interesting to notice what it was that turned the war
against Hitler. If it had not been this, it would doubtless
have been something else of the same general character.
Mussolini, when he was in Hitler's presence was fascinated
by him; but when he got back to Rome he felt humiliated
by his dependence upon him. He knew that although
Hitler was friendly to him, he did not trust him — and did
not hesitate to win some victories at his expense, as in the
case of the Balkan countries. He felt that Hitler was exploiting him — which he was. So he determined to do a
little adventuring on his own — without consulting Hitler.
This led to his campaign in Greece, from which Hitler had
to rescue him just at the moment when *he* (Hitler) was
completing his preparations for the invasion of Russia.
Hitler was overextended. Thus, his perfidious dealings
with his ally brought about his undoing. Not, however,

until he had brought unparalleled disaster to his country and the world. The fact that evil means can only bring about evil ends may be reassuring to our faith in justice as the law of God, but it brings no comfort when we remember that the evil ends contrived by tyrants can engulf us all.

There is no magic of history that makes the United States immune to tyranny if the people will not resist its encroachments. There is nothing that will save us from its evils, once it is established. Men of tyrannous purpose have already gone a long way, spreading fear far and wide through the land, accusing the innocent, intimidating the loyal, and through persecution have risen to power. If " goodness dare not check " them, they will follow the pattern of other tyrants and involve us all in measureless disaster.

Let us remember, ere it be too late, that the time to deal with tyranny is before it is entrenched.

PART THREE

THE RETREAT FROM THE FOUNDING PRINCIPLES

11. Must Freedom Protect Its Enemies?

Whenever it is pointed out that the methods of the current investigations transgress American judicial principles and infringe upon the civil rights which are the very core of our national inheritance, it is protested that Communists are not entitled to the protection that the rest of us may claim, since they are conspiring to overthrow the system of government that provides it. Shall they be given the freedom to destroy freedom? Must we allow them to use for their own purposes the rights that they would extinguish as soon as they had the power?

This protest should be carefully examined. It cannot lightly be brushed aside. For it is undoubtedly true that Communists are using our freedom with the intent of destroying it, and equally true that they would deny to others the rights they insist upon for themselves. The notion, held by some, that a free society is bound by its principles to give the shelter of its civil rights to a conspiracy against the society itself, *even if the conspiracy is succeeding,* is insupportable.

However, let the italicized clause be fully noted. As we shall see later, the restriction of freedom in order to protect it from its enemies all too easily becomes the withdrawal of freedom from its friends. Similarly, rights suspended because they are being abused are soon lost to the entire society.

The most, therefore, that we can concede is that *if a free society is in genuine danger* from those who are using its freedoms to undermine the society itself, the rights of the conspirators must be curtailed *to whatever extent is actually necessary* for the security of the free society. Again, let the emphasis be noted. For the curtailment of rights in *any* circumstances is fraught with peril. This peril must therefore be kept at the absolute minimum.

What the situation amounts to is that freedom is not obliged to commit suicide. If a condition exists — as it has in some countries — in which a Communist conspiracy is attempting to take over the government illegally, the legal government is entitled to take whatever measures are necessary to put down the conspiracy. It would have been entirely appropriate, for example, in some of the countries which the Communist minority was allowed to take over, if the government representing the non-Communist majority had expelled the Communists from the legislature — and from the cabinet, if they were in it — and thereupon had tried them for treason. This would have been justified even though the Communists thus treated had been legally elected. There *is* a point — and it is blind and foolish to deny it — where the law of necessity takes over.

To take an example with Communism left out of it — which may be a good thing to do for the purpose of clear thinking — we can imagine a community in which the people are all starving but in which one wealthy man has stored for himself a great quantity of food which he is unwilling to share. The law of necessity would *not* be in conflict with moral law if the community seized the wealthy man's store of food and distributed it, even though this would be illegal. It would be necessary, however — to com-

plete the illustration — for the community to make restitution to the man whose possessions it had forcibly seized,
whenever it acquired the means of doing so. And this
would be the case, no matter how low an opinion the
community had of this man, or how richly he deserved it.
For the law of necessity must be applied only to the extent
essential. Otherwise, restraints would disappear and civilized values be in jeopardy.

There are also other ways in which a free society — and
its citizens — need not allow themselves to be trapped by a
perversely literalistic application of its values. Here, for instance, is a man who comes to ask me to sign a petition. I
read it and recognize that I am in formal agreement with its
terms. Am I therefore morally obliged to sign it? The
man who has brought it to me says that I am. "No," I
reply, "I think I am not — because this petition is not
brought to me in good faith. It will be used for purposes
with which I profoundly disagree. In short, this petition
was framed by Communists to serve a Communist purpose and I shall not sign it."

"Then, you are going back on your convictions," objects
the man. "You are not willing to put your name to what
you have repeatedly said that you believe. What sort of
moral position is that?"

"It is a very strong moral position," I tell him. "It is
the position of not allowing good ends to be perverted
into bad ones. It is the position of not obeying the devil
when he appears as an angel of light. It is the position of
emphatically *not* supposing that because you want to be
good, you have to be stupid. Fidelity to a principle is
fidelity not merely to what that principle formally commands but fidelity to its intention. In this case which you

have brought before me, the intention of the principle which you want me to mis-apply is quite definitely *not* to serve the stratagems of the Communist Party."

It is highly important, as it seems to me, that all who love freedom and defend traditional American rights shall define their stand in realistic terms, making clear their awareness of Communist imposture and treachery, and showing that they are unwilling to be thoughtless and un-critical in applying their principles. For no action is really moral that is taken upon the basis of precept only and with-out regard to its consequences.

We repeat, therefore: a free society is not obliged to extend its protection to conspirators *to the point where the society and its freedoms are endangered.*

But what is our present situation in America? There is no slightest doubt of the threat of Communism from abroad or that it places us in deadly danger. There is no doubt but that there are spies and saboteurs within the United States, and perhaps other agents of the Commu-nist cause, under orders from the Soviet Union and working under Party discipline. It is clear that these enemies must be identified, and either apprehended and punished or — if it be to our national advantage — left free for a while and kept under surveillance. This is the concern of the FBI and of whatever other agencies are established by the ap-propriate departments of the government.

There is no *need*, however, to curb the civil rights of Communists engaged in treason. They can have all the protection our judicial system affords, and yet, if the evi-dence is plain, they will be found guilty and justly con-victed. In other words, no case can be made out for the curtailment of civil liberties or the adoption of methods of investigation repugnant to our judicial procedures on the basis that there are Communists who are committing treason. Such Communists can be effectually tried in our courts in accordance with our traditions.

If it be contended — as it is by apologists for the Congressional committees — that this leaves everything to a Department of Justice which is not to be trusted to prosecute such cases, the answer is that if so serious a charge is really substantial, the Congressional committees should investigate the Department of Justice. Actually, most of us will not easily be persuaded that the Department of Justice, which contains the FBI, is poorly informed, or that it is not eager to take energetic action in cases of treason.

The one case to which the Congressional committees keep pointing as evidence of their usefulness is that of Alger Hiss. But the fact is that in this matter the Committee on Un-American Activities is entirely indebted to Whittaker Chambers who withheld from the Department of Justice *for many years* important documentary evidence upon which it would have been bound to act. The publicity-seeking Un-American Activities Committee merely reaped the reward of Mr. Chambers' delay — highly discreditable to Mr. Chambers himself and casting grave doubt upon his probity and the sincerity of his motivation — in disclosing to the government what he was under obligation to disclose much earlier. Moreover, the Un-American Activities Committee was taken by surprise when, owing to Mr. Chambers' unexpectedly sensational revelations, the case took the turn it did. This is proved by the fact that Mr. Nixon, the member of the committee most concerned in the investigation, had taken a trip abroad, from which he hastily returned by airplane when he discovered that his complacency may have been ill-founded.

The Congressional committees, however, have had no other case like that of Mr. Hiss. To the extent that they are concerned with people who may be Communists, they are investigating not espionage or contemplated sabotage or the activities of agents of the Communist conspiracy, but persons who are described, rightly or wrongly, as holding Communist or pro-Communist opinions. From this, they have extended their investigation — and here we come to what they are really pursuing — to those who are believed to have had, at some time in the past, either hopeful views of Communism itself or views of public issues which Communists were also said to hold. And these people are accused of having been sufficiently close to the Communist conspiracy to have forfeited the right to the protection of traditional American procedures.[1]

As to the procedures which the committees have substituted for the traditional American ones, they have been accurately described by Agnes E. Meyer as " of a character to make any honest American sick to his stomach, regardless of whether he thinks the victim may be or may have been a fellow-traveller. I have seen only one sight to compare with it," she continues, " a Spanish bull fight where half a dozen men stick sharp knives into the bull to enrage him before the matador — or in this case the committee chairman — closes in for the kill." [2]

What possible excuse is there for this departure from

---

[1] Such procedures as the Grand Jury to determine whether the case shall go to trial, the presumption of innocence until guilt is proven, confrontation of witnesses, cross-examination on behalf of the accused, and all that centuries of experience have built up into the wisdom and humanity of Anglo-American justice.

[2] Address before the American Association of School Administrators, Atlantic City, N. J., February 17, 1953.

American traditions of justice and fair play? As we have conceded, if a free society is in genuine danger from those who are using its freedoms to undermine the society itself, the rights of individuals may need to be curtailed to whatever extent is actually necessary for the security of the free society. But those who are haled before the Congressional committees do not represent this sort of threat, even the ones who may have Communist sympathies.

If indeed they do have Communist sympathies and are in one way or another taking advantage of American freedom to advance opinions which belong to the Communist system of ideas, they can be answered in the open forum; if they are working in a free institution such as a university, it is the concern of that institution to deal with them in accordance with its rules. Should it happen that the government has exclusive evidence of the Communist activity of such a person, the evidence can be made available to the institution concerned. In any case, in the United States, we cannot afford that anyone shall be persecuted, even a Communist-sympathizer, *for his opinions.* Conspiracy is one thing; opinion another. We have a Department of Justice to deal with conspiracy — as with all other unlawful behavior; but no department of the government should be dealing with matters of opinion.

The truth is that the threat of Communism within the United States, so far as it has to do with treasonable activities, can be fully met without modifying in any way our customary judicial procedure. So far as it has to do with activities which are not illegal, such as the promotion of Communist ideas, it is not a serious threat and in no way excuses the excesses of the investigating committees.[3]

[3] Membership in the Communist Party had shrunk, by the end of 1951, to a third of what it was during the war.

A much greater evil is the unjust and oppressive behavior of the committees towards people who are not and never have been Communists but whose views the committees do not like. The excuse given by the committees — and their apologists — that the threat of Communism justifies the suspension of the traditional American respect for human rights is, in these cases, not only utterly unfounded but downright irrelevant.

As Jefferson told us long ago, once we begin on this path we are forfeiting our freedoms. " Subject opinion to coercion: whom will you make your inquisitors? Fallible men; men governed by bad passions, by private as well as public reasons. And why subject it to coercion? To produce uniformity." [4] That is what we have! Fallible men: men whose ambition, whose passion for publicity, whose private rather than public reasons drive them to persecute those of differing views — people who are seldom Communists but who, through reckless assertion and inquisitorial procedure, can be made to seem so to the public.

To sum up, freedom *can* — and indeed *must* — protect itself from its enemies, including those on the committees. But freedom, if its friends are still to possess it, must not be curtailed because enemies which cannot seriously harm it are abusing it.

The distinction which the American people must learn to make is between active conspirators against their free society and those who hold unpopular — and even repugnant — opinions. Unless freedom protects enemies of the latter sort who are not truly perilous to it — protects them, that is to say, by permitting them the same civil rights that are claimed for the society as a whole — the danger is that

[4] T. Jefferson, *Notes on Virginia*, 1782.

freedom will not be able to protect its friends. That is what is happening in the United States at the present time.

As Judge Learned Hand, one of the most humane and literate jurists of our time, has summarized it: " Risk for risk, for myself I had rather take my chance that some traitors will escape detection than spread abroad a spirit of general suspicion and distrust which accepts rumor and gossip in place of undismayed and unintimidated inquiry. I believe that that community is already in process of dissolution where each man begins to eye his neighbor as a possible enemy, where non-conformity with the accepted creed, political as well as religious, is a mark of disaffection; where denunciation, without specification or backing, takes the place of evidence; where orthodoxy chokes freedom of dissent; where faith in the eventual supremacy of reason has become so timid that we dare not enter our convictions in the open lists to win or lose. Such fears as these are a solvent which can eat out the cement that binds the stones together; they may in the end subject us to a despotism as evil as any that we dread; and they can be allayed only insofar as we refuse to proceed on suspicion, and trust one another until we have tangible ground for misgiving. The mutual confidence on which all else depends can be maintained only by an open mind and a brave reliance upon free discussion. I do not say that these will suffice; who knows but we may be on a slope which leads down to aboriginal savagery. But of this I am sure: if we are to escape, we must not yield a foot in demanding a fair field, and an honest race, for all ideas." [5]

[5] Address before the 86th Convention of the University of the State of New York, Albany, October 24, 1952.

12. The Attack on Freedom of Opinion

All persecutors, before they go very far with their careers, become concerned at what is being said about them and want to control it. In a free society, this means that they collide with the principle of freedom of opinion. They are, of course, unfriendly to this principle in any case, since it makes it difficult for their own opinions to hold the field unchallenged, but it is likely to be its threat to their immediate personal fortunes that first precipitates the issue.

We have seen this demonstrated unmistakably in the behavior of Senator McCarthy. When the *Capital Times* of Madison, Wisconsin, disclosed some of the Senator's financial transactions, he not only implied that the newspaper was pro-Communist ("closer to the *Daily Worker* than any other newspaper in the country"), but urged the Milwaukee Retail Food Dealers to withdraw their advertising so as not to contribute "to bringing the Communist Party line into the homes of Wisconsin." (The *Capital Times* is, in fact, a strongly anti-Communist newspaper and had led the fight to purge Milwaukee's labor unions of Communist influence.) [6]

When a well-known columnist and radio commentator

[6] See *McCarthy: The Man, the Senator, the "Ism,"* by Jack Anderson and Ronald W. May (Boston: Beacon Press, 1952), pp. 272 ff.

printed unfavorable reports about him, the Senator brought pressure to bear — successfully — upon his radio sponsor to decline to renew his contract.[7]

When *Time* magazine, after a period of aloofness, lost its patience and pointed out that McCarthy had not identified a single Communist in the government in spite of his extravagant claims, the Senator felt that he had "a duty to let [the] advertisers know" that they may be unknowingly "flooding American homes with Communist Party line material" if they "continue to advertise in *Time* magazine after they know what *Time* is doing."[8]

Similarly, the Senator threatened a law-suit against publishers who had reprinted a Senate Subcommittee Report on the McCarthy financial transactions, the original government edition of which became strangely difficult to purchase.[9] Most recently, he has "investigated," in secret hearing, a newspaper editor who had been bold enough to give his readers his undisguised opinion of the Senator;[10] and at the time of this writing, he is indicating to another newspaper editor,[11] who evaluated the "investigation" of the first one with unfaltering devotion to the highest standards of newspaper ethics, that newspapers, when they go through the mails, pay postage at a rate which is subject to increase. He did not, however, make it plain how the postage rates applying to this particular newspaper were to

[7] The columnist: Drew Pearson; the sponsor: the Adam Hat Co.; the charge against Pearson: that he is a "Communist spokesman"; the fact: Pearson has been consistently anti-Communist. (He was the first, for example, to make known the facts about the Russian spy ring in Canada.)

[8] Anderson and May, *op. cit.*, pp. 277 ff.

[9] Report of the Subcommittee on Privileges and Elections, *op. cit.*

[10] Editor James A. Wechsler of the *New York Post*; neither he nor Mrs. Sooneborn, his publisher, was intimidated.

[11] J. Russell Wiggins, Managing Editor of the *Washington Post*.

be raised without the same new rates applying to other newspapers.[12]

If we turn to the collision of the Un-American Activities Committee with the principle of freedom of opinion, we see (in this one matter of its threat to the immediate political fortunes of " investigators ") a somewhat different approach. When Bishop G. Bromley Oxnam, like myself and others, criticized the methods of the Committee, Mr. Jackson of California, a Committee member much too intelligent not to know what he was doing, made an attack on the Bishop (under the shelter of Congressional immunity) charging him with serving " the Communist front." This attack, like the release of unevaluated material from the Committee's files, was intended to place the Bishop on the defensive, so that he would express his opinions less freely.

The fact is that it is of the highest importance to the public welfare that the methods of this Committee be vigorously debated. One of the most restrained evaluations of it that has yet appeared comes from the pen of an English jurist, the Earl Jowitt, former Lord Chancellor and Attorney General of Great Britain. Although, as a foreigner, his statement will be viewed by many as intrusive, others will welcome it for its detachment. " I feel

[12] Mr. Philip Graham, the Publisher of the *Post*, has indicated that he is not responsive to threats to raise the postal rates. " We do not agree," he says in a published statement, " with Senator McCarthy that newspapers should be compliant to a Senator's demands just because the Congress has voted mail rates that may provide a subsidy to newspapers. We have consistently stated in our editorials that newspapers should be charged the full cost of mail service by the Postoffice. It is obvious to us that any receipt of Government favors raises the precise threat to freedom of the press which is now openly declared in Senator McCarthy's letter. Senator McCarthy has given no evidence that he is qualified to become Chief Censor of what news may be sent in the mail." (*Washington Post*, August 22, 1953.)

bound to say," he writes, " that the luckless individual who appears before such a committee may find himself rather in the position of the shuttlecock between two expert wielders of the battledore. If it be true that political considerations are to influence the conduct of such a committee, if he is to be used as the *corpus vile* whereby the legislative branch is to put pressure on the executive branch to activate the judicial branch, his lot is indeed unhappy. The administration of justice and the participation in political life are surely two useful and praiseworthy activities. It is a mere platitude to say that they should be kept, so far as possible, in watertight compartments, for when politics comes in by the door justice tends to fly out by the window." [13]

Earl Jowitt also reminds us that Whittaker Chambers, in his book, *Witness*, describes the " mute gloom " of the Committee when the Hiss investigation was not going as the Committee members wished. " We're ruined," one of them said, and Chambers describes this lament as justified at the time since it was an election year and the seat of every member was at stake. The terrible implication of this, which the American people have seldom fully grasped, is that a quasi-judicial Committee, armed with the power of Congress, proceeds to " try " witnesses, not with the impartial aim of discovering their innocence or guilt but with the purpose of making their " conviction," if it can be brought about, or seem to be, politically useful in furthering the careers of the Committee members.

Those who, in the interest of traditional American justice, desire to make this situation plain will, however, like

[13] The Earl Jowitt, *The Strange Case of Alger Hiss* (N.Y.: Doubleday & Co., 1953), p. 145.

Bishop Oxnam, be resented and excoriated. The freedom to speak out, since it cannot at present be limited more directly, is placed under as much constraint as possible by the threat of false accusation and damage to reputation.

It is time, however, that we examined the principle of freedom of opinion itself. It is the *basic* freedom: in its absence all other freedoms are unprotected and illusory. It may be defined most simply as the right of the individual to hold whatever opinions he will, and the right to express them freely. It is because they understood completely the primacy of this principle and its indispensability to a free society, that those who shaped our early history increasingly insisted upon its firm establishment, and finally wrote it into the Bill of Rights to place it under the guardianship of the Constitution.

Historically — to enter now upon a brief summary — the struggle for freedom of opinion centered upon two issues: liberty of conscience in religious belief and the right to criticize the government. In both cases, there was a long and bitter conflict, beginning in Europe — chiefly England — and fought through to the point of their establishment as foundational American principles.

The story of the religious struggle is fairly well known: first, Catholics and Protestants contending for sole authority as the State Church of England; then Anglicans and Nonconformists, the former fighting for exclusive recognition, the latter for toleration; then, the New England attempt at theocracy — and its failure; finally, the gathering impulse which led to the recognition of freedom of belief and the separation of Church and State acknowledged in the First Amendment to the Constitution.

"Congress shall make no law," reads this amendment (adopted December 15, 1791), "respecting an establishment of religion, or prohibiting the free exercise thereof." Eleven years earlier, in the Virginia Statute of Religious Freedom (1779), Thomas Jefferson had written, "All men shall be free to profess, and by argument to maintain, their opinion in matters of religion; and . . . the same shall in no wise diminish, enlarge, or affect their civil capacities." In a letter to the Baptist Chamber of Virginia, in May, 1789, George Washington had said, "Every man, conducting himself as a good citizen, and being accountable to God alone for his religious opinions, ought to be protected in worshipping the Deity according to the dictates of his own conscience."

Testimony, however, is scarcely necessary. Freedom of opinion in religion, although still assailed by those who would supplant it with their own authority, is incontestibly an American founding principle.

But so, also, is freedom of the press. Here, too, there was a long, hard struggle. Printers in England were repeatedly punished for publishing reports about public issues and opinions about the government. Lord Chief Justice Scroggs, in 1679, had held it criminal at the common law to "write on the subject of government, whether in terms of praise or censure, it is not material, for no man has a right to say anything of government."

This same contention was put forward by Lord Howard of Effingham, when he arrived in Virginia in 1684; indeed, he went further, proclaiming that "no person be permitted to use any press for printing upon any occasion whatsoever." And even as late as 1719, the Pennsylvania legislature warned an offending printer "not to print anything again on government." [14]

In the case of the press, like that of religion, the struggle for freedom eventuated in a Constitutional guarantee: "Congress shall make no law abridging the freedom of speech or of the press." Here, too, though by many it is not as well known or seems to have been forgotten, the Founding Fathers were perfectly clear that freedom of opinion is the basic freedom and that, at all costs, it must be maintained if other freedoms are to endure.

"Where the press is free and every man able to read," wrote Jefferson, "all is safe." "This formidable censor of the public functionaries," he continued, "by arraigning them at the tribunal of public opinion, produces reform peaceably, which must otherwise be done by revolution." [15] Again, in a letter to George Washington (1792), he wrote, "No government ought to be without censors; and where the press is free, none ever will."

"The liberty of the press," said Alexander Hamilton, in a speech in New York City in 1804, includes the liberty to publish the truth even "though it reflect on the government, on magistrates, or individuals." "The press shall be free to every citizen," states the Constitution of the State of Delaware (1782), "who undertakes to examine the official conduct of men acting in a public capacity, and any citizen may print freely on any subject, being responsible for the abuse of that liberty."

Academic freedom — which is freedom to transmit knowl-

[14] Quoted from an address, "The Printed Word," by J. R. Wiggins, Managing Editor of the *Washington Post*, at the Maryland Library Association, May 9, 1953. (It is interesting to see McCarthy's charges against Mr. Wiggins against the background of the above history.)
[15] Letter to Charles Yancey, 1816.

edge and explore opinions without being bound by dogma or required to arrive at preconceived conclusions — was inherited from the English universities and is expressed as much in the exploring spirit of Franklin and Priestley as in Jefferson's defiance of " every sort of tyranny over the mind of man." Its Constitutional safeguard is the First Amendment. It is true that it has not been as frequently or as clearly formulated as is the case with religion and the press, but ever since colonial days when the earliest American universities were founded, the spirit of freedom of inquiry has been the academic equivalent of the spirit of independence in religion and in the press. Certainly, pressure for conformity is just as repugnant to the founding principles in the case of education as in any other.

This, then, is our heritage, the basic American liberty, achieved by centuries of struggle, and the nurture and protection of all other liberties. And this is the liberty that the persecutors fear and hate — as they have always done — and, little by little, are trying to stifle and suppress.

It is always " little by little." As James Madison warned us, " There are more instances of abridgment of the freedom of the people by gradual and silent encroachments of those in power than by violent and sudden usurpations." [16]

Yet, we have already gone a long way. Anyone who defends *in actual situations* the traditional American liberty which I have just defined is viewed with suspicion. To hold, as the Founding Fathers did, that freedom of opinion is the basis of our national life, and then to apply this principle to schools and colleges, is " being soft to Communists." To plead that academic freedom is essential to the growth of healthy minds is advocating that " subver-

[16] Speech in the Virginia Convention, June 16, 1788.

sives " be protected in our educational system. To believe
that American ideas can stand their ground in free debate
is close to treason. To be a patriot, one must assume that
American principles are not defensible in open argument
and that " Communist notions," unless suppressed would
prove invincible. A " good " American is thus a frightened
American whose loyalty is measured by his fear of his an-
tagonist's ideas — which have terrified him with their intellectual potency!

All this is fantasy. It must be exposed for what it is:
a renunciation of our democratic faith and a subversion
of our freedom. Nothing makes it necessary; nothing ever
could. The fact that there are Communists — at most, a
very small percentage — in our schools and colleges does
not justify widespread intimidation in the name of investigation. If there are Communist teachers who are actively
conspiring against the peace and security of the people of
the United States, let the Department of Justice apprehend
them. There is no American freedom, and could not possibly be, that gives shelter to conspiracy. But when the
charge is made, let it be one of conspiracy. For there *is*
an American freedom which protects opinion — even disagreeable opinion. The charge should never be that an
individual holds Marxist views, because, whatever the rest
of us may think about such views, the principle that protects all Americans is the freedom of each to hold whatever
views he will. Any surrender of this principle, on any
ground whatever, is always perilous, for to surrender on
one ground means presently to yield on others.

That is what has happened already. Those chiefly affected by Congressional investigations of our educational
system are not Communists but teachers who are becoming

afraid to take up, even for exploration, adventurous or non-conforming views which may be used for manufacturing a case against them. These are the teachers most injured — and their students with them.

As to the teachers for whom the investigators say they are searching, if there are teachers who have lost their independence because they are under Communist Party discipline and therefore cannot teach in accordance with the standards of their profession, they should be made answerable to the faculty to which they have brought dishonor, and to the governing boards of their institutions. The government has nothing whatever to do with the matter — except in cases of conspiracy.

Even the faculties, of course, must be on their guard lest, in the present atmosphere of phobia and tension, they confuse the non-conformist with the Communist, the innocent with the guilty. And they should remember that, although in the *world situation* Communism is the enemy, in the *conflict of opinion* Communist ideas, although inimical, are not a serious threat. No matter what the lists of allegedly Communist and pro-Communist teachers which from time to time are produced — and which, for our present purpose, it is not necessary to evaluate — the fact is that not many students are joining the Communist Party. Nor, in any case, do any but the most exceptional people join it because of the attractiveness of Communist ideas. They join it to meet an emotional need.[17]

The real danger is not that our youth will be indoctrinated with Communism but that we shall produce a generation of intellectual " sissies." As I have already suggested, we are making Marxist doctrine seem so potent that

[17] See Chapter 7: " What Makes a Communist? "

no one who is exposed to it can hope to resist it. This is sheer stupidity. Our young people need to know what they are fighting — and that they can defeat it. They need to understand Communism with clear, unsheltered minds.

To win the struggle for the future, they will need to persuade the undecided millions of a world in spiritual ferment that Communism is wrong and democracy right. They cannot do this if they do not know what Communism is and how it gains a hold on people. Their battle will be against Communism's strength rather than its weakness. To win this battle, they must themselves be strong in confidence, and confidence cannot grow in an atmosphere of intimidation.

Unbridled investigation, undertaken by men who do not understand academic freedom and are not sympathetic to it, will do incalculable harm to education. Non-conforming opinions can be labelled Communist even though they are directly opposed to Communism. The intelligent discussion of the crucial issues which only the informed can understand, including the issues between ourselves and the Kremlin, will be hopelessly impaired. An attempt will be made to expel the " controversial " subject from the curriculum and the " controversial " teacher from the faculty, even though controversy is the very essence of robust and healthy education.

It is not only in the educational system and in the newspapers, however, that freedom of opinion is being invaded. It is being invaded everywhere. As we have seen in recent months (spring and early summer of 1953), even the churches are not immune. It is true that committee members go out of their way to make a distinction between churches and churchmen, but this is utterly misleading. If a churchman who holds progressive views, applying the insights of religion to social problems, is haled before a committee and made to appear to be pro-Communist while actually he is deeply opposed to Communism, this is not only false witness at its most wicked: it quite definitely does impugn — and on a spurious and fraudulent basis — the ethical aims and socially redemptive purposes of churches. It also burdens — and consciously or unconsciously, this is the end the committee has in view — the freedom of churches to hold social ideals and to express them.[18]

But as well as churches, the actual religious beliefs of individuals can apparently be brought into question — in spite of the Constitutional prohibition against it. At a hearing before the Permanent Subcommittee on Investigations of the Senate, March 2, 1953, presided over by Senator McCarthy, Mr. Lyons, the Director of Religious Programming of the Voice of America, was asked repeatedly to describe his religious beliefs. Although he told the Committee in a prepared statement (which he ought never to have felt required to present) that he believed in God, he was minutely examined as to whether this belief had been made apparent in dissertations and academic papers he had prepared during his post-graduate work.[19]

[18] The very patient reader who wants to analyze the psychology of a committee hearing as to this matter can do no better than to study the record of Bishop Oxnam's hearing before the Un-American Activities Committee, Tuesday, July 21, 1953.

[19] Official Report of the Hearing, Part 4, pp. 298 ff. (Parenthetically, it may be mentioned that none of the Senators present were equipped to understand, in theological terms, the questions they were asking. What would they have done, for example, if Professor Paul Tillich's affirmation of a " God beyond God " had been taken up? And yet, Professor Tillich, besides being a foremost theologian capable of adventurous ideas, works within the Christian system. The Senators were not even able to understand the witness's reference to Dr. Carl Jung's school of Analytical Psy-

None of these questions were the Senators (Jackson and McClellan as well as McCarthy) entitled to ask. The Constitution expressly forbids it. (Article 6, last paragraph: " No religious test shall ever be required as a qualification to any office or public trust under the United States.") How far we are moving in the wrong direction in this respect is dramatically illustrated by a letter of Thomas F. Bayard, Secretary of State in the Cleveland administration, to Baron Ignatz von Schaeffer, Austro-Hungarian Minister to the United States. The letter is dated May, 1885, and includes the following: " It is not within the power of the President, nor of Congress, nor of any judicial tribunal of the United States, to take or even hear testimony, or in any mode to inquire into or decide upon the religious belief of any official."

We have moved a long way since then. Men who not only hold the Constitution in contempt but who are disdainful of all the ethical values of the Judeo-Christian tradition are stealing from the American people, little by little, their heritage and their honor. In the words of William T. Evjue, Editor and Publisher of the *Capital Times* of Madison, Wisconsin:

" Today, Communism has become the perfect scareword with which the entrenched order can club the American people into submission and conformity. Millions of peo-

---

chology. Under their prodding, he gave this name to the category of modern psychology, stemming from Freud but deviant from orthodox Freudianism, which is associated with Dr. Jung. But the Senators insisted upon the " School " being housed in some sort of building in Switzerland and having a known number of pupils working formally for academic credit. They are not to be blamed for their ignorance of a field of study to which they are strangers (though it is a field that explains more about politics and politicians than they might wish to realize!) if only they would recognize their limitations, both academic and by constitutional restriction, and abide by them.

ple have been denied the right of free speech through fear of being branded as disloyal. The press, radio, television and the movies have cringed before the assault that has been made on the printed and the spoken word. Boycott has been urged by the political demagogues who have sought to still criticism by threatening to pin the label of Communism on an offender. Confidence of the people in their government has been threatened by casting the shadow of disloyalty over thousands of honest and conscientious persons. A campaign of hate, suspicion, distrust, confusion and character assassination has been let loose at a time when there is a great need for unity, confidence and a united front to meet a world menace." [20]

Nowhere more than in the suppression of freedom of opinion has this campaign succeeded in robbing us of the traditional values that our Fathers cherished. Let us be clear about it. The Fathers were not merely theorists. They knew the bitter taste of history. We too may know it — if we let things drift until it is too late.

[20] Address at the Hotel Biltmore, New York, September 25, 1952, in connection with the Prize Award of the Sidney Hillman Foundation.

13. What Is an Un-American?

The purpose of the Un-American Activities Committee, as described in the law under which it operates is " to
make from time to time investigations of (i) the extent,
character, and objects of un-American propaganda activities in the United States, (ii) the diffusion within the
United States of subversive and un-American propaganda
that is instigated from foreign countries or of a domestic
origin and attacks the principle of the form of government
as guaranteed by our Constitution, and (iii) all other questions in relation thereto that would aid Congress in any
necessary remedial legislation." [21]

It will be noted that the term " subversive " appears to
be defined by the clause following and means anything
that " attacks the principle of the form of government as
guaranteed by our Constitution," and if this were the only
term used, the authorization would be fairly clear. But to
the term " subversive " is added another word — " un-
American " — which is not defined at all.

The Committee has been with us for a long time now —
it was first authorized in 1936 — but it has yet to tell us
what is meant by " un-American." With each new Congress, its members have come and gone — some back to
private life, others to higher office, one to jail — but none

[21] Public Law 601, 79th Congress (1946), chapter 753, 2nd session;
repeated in Rules Adopted by the 83rd Congress, House Resolution 5,
January 3, 1953.

of them has given us a definition. The first chairman, Martin Dies, did say as the Committee was about to begin its work, "We might jeopardize fundamental rights far more important than the objective we seek," but he did not try to limit this danger by defining more particularly what the Committee's objective was intended to be.

Perhaps the best context in which to seek a definition, at any rate as a beginning, is that of asking how a similar adjective would sound if applied by some other nation. What, for instance, would be an un-French activity, or an un-Peruvian activity, or even an un-Eskimo activity? Would we take it as a matter of course if in Sweden, for example, there were set up a Committee on Un-Swedish Activities? Or (to come nearer home) in Canada, a Committee on Un-Canadian Activities? These comparisons are revealing: the word *un-American* quite evidently has a different and distinctive connotation.

If we ask ourselves the further question as to what countries *might* have such a committee, it will probably occur to us that a Committee on Un-Nazi Activities would have sounded quite natural in Hitler's Germany; and so would a Committee on Un-Communist Activities be unsurprising in the case of Russia and its satellites. The reason, of course, is not obscure.

The word *un-American,* like the words *un-Nazi* or *un-Communist,* has reference not only to a national territory and the national system located upon it, but to the whole contested territory of ways of life and to the struggle between systems of ideas. Americanism is opposed to Communism, as it was to Nazism, not only because the United States as an inhabited country is threatened by such movements but because Americanism is a rival movement.

As Justice Oliver Wendell Holmes once put it, "Not by aggression, but by the naked fact of existence, the United States is an eternal danger and an unsleeping threat to every government that founds itself upon anything but the will of the governed." In other words, unlike most other countries, the United States by its very nature is a world influence, a world force.

This is not to say that the House of Representatives, in appointing the Committee on Un-American Activities, had this significance in view. But it does indicate that the name would have sounded awkward and impossible unless such a significance, whether understood or not, had been conferred by history. And therefore, it would not have been proposed or allowed.

But here, surely, is the very matter that we must explore. To know what the word *un-American* means, we must know what the word *American* means, and since it evidently has a meaning indicated by a special history, we must ask what this history is.

Nor is there any other starting-place. If it be said that an American is simply a person born in America, then clearly, since he cannot be born all over again somewhere else, he can never be anything but an American, no matter what his activities. Nor can his activities, whatever they are, be other than American, for American activities, on this rendering, would be any activities in which a person born in America cared to engage. Such a person, no matter what he did, could not be justly accused of un-American activities.

Nor, unless we wish to indict the Roman Catholic hierarchy, can we simplify the question by defining un-American activities as activities controlled by a foreign state. For the Roman Catholic hierarchy is controlled by the Vatican, and the Vatican is a foreign state.

It is the same if we think of un-American activities as friendliness to a foreign revolutionary movement. Thomas Jefferson was friendly to the French Revolutionary movement, at any rate until its excesses shocked him; and yet it is difficult to think of this as in itself an un-American activity, or of Jefferson as un-American.

It is obviously not a matter, then, of any of these simplified approaches. It must be something in the realm of ideas, something that tests behavior by a standard supported *by* ideas, and thus something that has a history.

What *is* this history? It began with the fact that the nation itself was founded upon a particular inheritance, derived from non-conformist English Protestantism, and from the philosophy of the natural rights of man as developed by John Locke, and from the supremacy of reason and justice declared by Voltaire, and from the French philosophical movement that followed: so that American democracy, as Irwin Edman has put it, is a " union of the ideas of natural justice and natural rights. . . . The notion of justice was classical and French; the concept of liberties was revolutionary and English." [22]

It was the ferment of these ideas that evolved the principles avowed in the Declaration of Independence: the principles of equal liberties and equal natural rights. It was from these ideas, carried into action, that the American Revolution came, and the Constitution, and presently and very importantly, the Bill of Rights. Nor is the further evolution of these ideas to be marked only by such figures

[22] Irwin Edman, *Fountainheads of Freedom* (N.Y.: Reynal & Hitchcock, 1941), p. 138.

as Jefferson, Jackson and Lincoln, significant though they
are. It was not only " government of the people, by the
people, for the people "; it was also Emerson's doctrine of
the sacredness of the individual: the doctrine that has sometimes been called " the citizen as soul "; and it was Whitman's song of the citizen as brother and comrade. And
the vision of all of them that America had a mission for
the world.

If we suppose — and sometimes it *is* supposed — that
Americanism so defined existed only in the minds of a few
idealists, we are far astray. Not only did the people revere
the idealists — from Jefferson on — who held this view of
the mission of America, thereby authenticating their Americanism, but, as documented by such writers as Professor
Gabriel, even in the early days when the new nation had
barely begun, there was scarcely a July Fourth utterance
that did not exalt the American mission " of being a beacon, a God-given beacon, showing to the world what liberty might mean to the whole human race." [23]

It is in this history, then, that we begin to see what the
word *American* means. And it is from this that we see
how, even from the beginning, the new nation has been a
potent world influence, challenging all humanity with the
Revolution of the Rights of Man.

If, therefore, we are to define *un-American* *activities*
authentically, we must define them as *everything whatever*
that hinders the advance of liberty under law, or that be-
trays the equality of human rights, or that transgresses the
freedom of the individual conscience, or profanes the

---

[23] Ralph Henry Gabriel, *The Course of American Democratic Thought*
(N.Y.: Ronald Press, 1940), p. 22.

sacredness of human personality. We should have to define as un-American *all impairments of civil rights, all discrimination on account of race or creed.* And we should have to identify as un-American *whatever threatened not only the material security but the spiritual influence of the United States as a nation whose mission to the world is indicated in its founding principles.*

In the light of this definition, which emerges naturally and inevitably from our history, what must our judgment be of the persecuting temper and heedless behavior of the Committee on Un-American Activities? Presumably, the Committee members know their country's history — though it certainly cannot be said that they are imbued with it. Indeed, the impression is occasionally almost irresistible that some of them believe that the United States was founded rather recently and more or less in their own constituencies. And the one un-American activity with which they are concerned is Communism within the United States — not abroad where it is most threatening to us, both militarily and politically, or where it is competing with us in the backward areas, but in our own country which is not in the least likely to turn Communist and where, as we have repeatedly seen, the chief protection needed is that of the FBI against spies and saboteurs.

The fact is, however, that even in dealing with Communism in the United States, the Committee has not concentrated on its task. Ernst and Loth, in preparing their *Report on the American Communist,* collected " several times more histories than the Congressional Committees have exposed in the last dozen years," the reason being that " the Committee did not try very hard; they were not interested in the former Communist except as an informer and scapegoat." [24] Their (Ernst and Loth's) verdict on the Committee's thirteen years of work is that " as a sounding board for professional harriers of dissent, who like to brand everyone they disagree with as Communist, and as an example, for the most part, of how not to combat Communism, the Committee has had no equal." [25]

This seems to be a correct verdict. The Committee's interest and energy have been chiefly expended on the persecution of anti-Communist liberals with profoundly American convictions: as in the recent cases of Agnes Meyer, who was falsely accused of having written a pro-Soviet letter in 1947, and Bishop G. Bromley Oxnam, who was outrageously charged with serving " God on Sunday and the Communist front for the balance of the week." But then, the chairman of the Committee, Mr. Harold Velde of Illinois, had already stated that " It's a lot better to wrongly accuse one person of being a Communist than to allow so many to get away." [26] This is the same Mr. Velde who, in 1952, introduced a bill in the House of Representatives that would have required the Librarian of Congress to read all the books in the Library — numbering more than nine million — and mark subversive material for the guidance of other libraries!

To return to our question — What is an un-American? — as we look at the record of this Committee, we feel at times that we are warm on the scent.

We remember that it was the Inquisition that directed that an individual could be seized on the information of

[24] Ernst and Loth, *op. cit.*, p. 25.
[25] *Ibid.*, p. 46.
[26] *Congressional Report* (published by the National Committee for an Effective Congress) March 6, 1953.

anyone whatever, no matter how infamous or criminal; that when brought before his inquisitors, this victim could be tried in secret and denied an advocate to defend him; and that the name of his accuser was not necessarily made known to him. We would call the Inquisition un-American.

We remember some of our fellow-citizens who have been rather confused about Americanism in the recent past. Mayor Hague of Jersey City, for example, who said to the Chamber of Commerce of that city, on January 12, 1938, the following words: " We hear about constitutional rights, free speech and the free press. Every time I hear those words I say to myself, ' That man is a Red, that man is a Communist.' You never heard a real American talk in that manner."

This statement is probably unmatched, and perhaps unmatchable, in its candor. But it is quite representative of those who, as described by Elmer Davis, " in the name of anti-Communism . . . try to strike down the freedom of the mind, which above all things differentiates us from the Communists; [who] in the name of Americanism . . . try to suppress the right to think what you like and say what you think, in the evident conviction — in so far as they have any reasoned conviction at all — that the principles on which this Republic was founded and has been operated will not bear examination." [27]

But it must not be conceded, and cannot be if we still have any respect for traditional American principles, that Communism is the sole business — even if honestly concentrated upon — of an Un-American Activities Committee. That Communism is un-American is self-evident.

[27] *Harper's Magazine*, August, 1953, p. 29.

But so are many other things: activities that bring into contempt American justice, American civil rights, American liberties; activities that lessen our influence in the world by betraying our ideals at home. These also should be of interest to the Committee.

If this, however, is too much to ask, we might at least have a committee that could manage its business without damaging the reputations of the innocent; a committee American enough to be chivalrous in its treatment of those against whom there is nothing more than rumor or suspicion, and fair enough to give them a genuine chance, if there is any real question about them, to prove their loyalty without being badgered and harrassed and without harmful publicity.

Until the Committee can be as American as this, there is nothing it can do to help us in the fight against Communism except dissolve itself and go out of existence. Then there will be one less embarrassment; one less argument that Communists can use against us; one less blot on the American principles that true Americans are eager to uphold.

It may be best in any case if the Committee's unhappy career is terminated. Then, perhaps, another committee, more broadly based than this one and with fewer political axes to grind, can be formed of persons eminent in public life and better equipped to undertake so difficult a task. If so, perhaps the new committee would begin its work by defining for us what it means to be American. Then we shall understand a great deal better what is meant by un-American activities.

14. The Suborning of Loyalty

Loyalty, like love, cannot be coerced. It is of the heart. People can no more be frightened into loyalty than they can be brought to it by cajolery. Nor, if they are *dis*loyal, can they be readily brought to confess it. If dissimulation is on their side, they will play the part of deceivers. That is why it is useless to administer loyalty oaths.

What is "loyalty to one's country"? The words are soon spoken, but what is the meaning? It cannot be mere loyalty to a piece of territory: for the same acres of earth would be very different under different sorts of human administration. And if it be loyalty to a body of principles, a form of society, a way of life — there must be an inner conviction, unforced and spontaneous, that these principles, this social form, this way of living are infinitely precious. Here is a loyalty that one either has or has not, a part, either present or missing, of one's personal development, one's spiritual essence. How can men be tested for it? And what can be done if they lack it?

When such a position is stated, and the ground of it sought in American tradition, it is usual to go to Jefferson. "If there be any among us who would wish to dissolve this Union, or to change its republican form, let them stand undisturbed as monuments of the safety with which error of opinion may be tolerated where reason is left free to combat it." [28]   This is the classical American tradition: tolerance not only for its own sake, but tolerance as the bounty of unshaken confidence.

But, it will be said, our situation is such as Jefferson never contemplated. This is not quite true, since Jefferson experienced the Alien and Sedition Acts era.

Given due time for comprehension, Jefferson would have understood this situation. To the conspiracy, as such, he would have applied whatever repressive measures were necessary — that is to say, he would have been concerned for the apprehension of traitors who were actively plotting against the peace and security of the nation. But — who can doubt it? — he would have insisted, now as in the early nineteenth century, that " error of opinion " may be " tolerated where reason is left free to combat it." He certainly would not have thought that in our free institutions — the teaching profession, for instance — any who wished " to dissolve this Union " would be deterred from it by an oath of loyalty. Or that such a person, knowing the consequences of candor, would hesitate at perjury.

But then, as to this, Alexander Hamilton, in many ways the arch-antagonist of Jefferson, would back him up to the hilt. An oath of loyalty, said Hamilton, " substitutes for the established and legal mode of investigating crimes and inflicting forfeitures one that is unknown to the Constitution and repugnant to the genius of our law." [29]

Among other things, he went on, such oaths " invert the order of things," obliging a citizen to establish his innocence; and they hold out a " bribe to perjury." It could

---

[28] Inaugural Address, March 4, 1801.
[29] *Cummings v. Missouri*, 4 Wall. 277, 330–31 (1867).

not have been put more pithily! Those who are disloyal are at an advantage if they swear falsely to their loyalty: those who are loyal do not need an oath at all.

What barrier is an oath to a Communist? The instruction given to Communists in the teaching profession in 1937, when the Party still printed some of its instructions openly, was as follows: "The Party must take careful steps to see that all teacher comrades are given thorough education in the teaching of Marxism-Leninism. Only when teachers have really mastered Marxism-Leninism will they be able skilfully to inject it into their teaching at the least risk of exposure and at the same time to conduct struggles around the schools in a truly Bolshevik manner." [30]

The degree to which teachers could inject Marxism-Leninism into their teaching at present as compared with the 1930's, and still escape detection, is undoubtedly much reduced. The public, as well as the Party, has been educated in Marxist-Leninist methods, and keeps a sharp look-out for "skilfully injected" Communist propaganda. But however that may be, this much is certain: teachers who have learned perfidy along these lines will not boggle when it comes to loyalty oaths, but will take them "in a truly Bolshevik manner."

The oaths are therefore useless. Those who take them sincerely do not need to take them; those who swear falsely are no more loyal — or detectably *dis*loyal — than they were before.

The only good loyalty oath — or fairly good one — is

---

[30] *The Communist*, May, 1937; quoted by V. T. Thayer, *American Education under Fire* (N.Y.: Harpers, 1944), p. 162.

doubtless the one quoted by former Attorney-General Francis Biddle, in his book, *The Fear of Freedom*. It is the oath said to have been sworn by the subjects of the ancient King of Aragon, in the presence of their monarch, and goes as follows: " We, who are as good as you, swear to you, who are no better than we, to accept you as our king and sovereign lord, provided that you observe all our liberties and laws; but if not, then not." [31]

Meanwhile, what the present loyalty oaths achieve is nothing but offense and insult to loyal citizens who sense their inner meaning: namely, that loyalty is being made obsequious and subservient. The oaths are part of the pattern of fear, whereby those who would be masters of the people first make them yield to indiscriminate submission.

To what am I loyal when I am loyal to the United States? To those who would be the country's masters, the men of tyranny who would like to be judges of us all? To those who will say, " This man is loyal; he says what I wish "; but " That man must be suspected; he does not bow down before me "? It is the odor of this that makes loyalty oaths offensive. True loyalty is to the country's great traditions and its liberties. It is a free man's loyalty, buoyant and self-assured.

One might ask, however, a rather dark but not irrelevant question: What is the loyalty of a persecutor? Here is a man who has risen to power because he has concentrated upon one thing at the expense of all others: his

---

[31] An oath of a similar pattern would be appropriate for witnesses who are being investigated by Congressional committees. Such an oath, to be simple and honest, and also fairly complete, might phrase itself like this:

" I, a free citizen of the United States, whose government is his agent not his master, do swear to tell as much of the truth as this Committee does not prevent or distort and I will be responsive to the Committee's questions to the full extent of their accord with our liberties and laws."

own advancement. Will a time ever come when his own advancement — or at least his preservation — is not the one thing that commands his loyalty? In a crisis, what will he give to his country? Indeed, what does he mean by " his country "? The domain of his own privileges or the community and its welfare?

Suppose — and I regret the grimness of the illustration — the Communist enemy reached a point where his power surpassed our own. This, upon the basis of our present policy, is not impossible. Suppose, instead of attacking us, he offered us, under face-saving formulas, what amounted to physical safety at the expense of moral surrender? Where, then, would our super-patriots be? If they knew that, through appropriate negotiations, they could still wield authority — perhaps increase it — after the surrender, would they be loyal to their country and its civilized values — or to their own supposed preferment?

I am not answering this question, but I quite definitely am asking it. I am not answering it because I know the complexity of human nature and the continuing struggle of good and evil in the hearts of men too well to judge men in advance — and least of all to condemn them on the basis of conjecture. But I ask it because it is a question we should have in mind.

The transformation of an American persecutor into a Commissar could take place without much change in character or motivation. He himself might scarcely know the difference. We have in recent memory the " collaborationists " of Vichy France. They were not Nazi at the beginning; perhaps they were never Nazi. But to survive and keep their power — or to gain it — they served the Nazi purpose.

Surely, those who would die for freedom if the need arose must be defending freedom now; those who would perish before they would be enslaved — are they not those who have always stood for human rights? What reliance shall we place in those who trample freedom? What shall we expect of those who disregard the rights that loyalty requires them to observe?

Where was their loyalty ever — to their friends, their colleagues, their supporters? If they betrayed these, whom then will they not betray? Why should we trust them? What a man is, he is in his entire character. If he has been shifty, perfidious, untrustworthy, that is the kind of man he is. *And that will be the quality of his loyalty.* How can a man's loyalty be better than the man himself — better than what he is in mind and heart?

Loyalty in a democracy, and especially in the United States, can never be expressed through *bullyism.* I use the term *bullyism* rather than a term presently current because, as it seems to me, it is a much more accurate term than any " ism " named after a man who, for the time being, is a member of our legislature. He did not invent what he serves — this man, or any other like him, before or after. It has been with us all along. In times of stress, it reappears.

There was something of it in New England theocracy, more of it in Nativism, the Know-Nothings, the Ku Klux Klan, the Anti-Semitism of Father Coughlin. Now, we have it once more — at a much more dangerous time and, for the moment, in a more successful form. But it is the same old bullyism, applauded in the same old way, and by the same kinds of people.

I say " kinds " rather than " kind " of people because

they are not of one category. There are those, earlier described, who express their persecuting impulse vicariously through a bully: those who, through unhappy defects of personality, draw keen enjoyment out of "seeing people pushed around." [32] There are also those who regret the bullyism but condone it because they think — or try to think — that it serves a necessary purpose. This purpose is always identified with what is called American interest or "the American way of life," but it is really the self-interest of those concerned, short-sighted and narrowly conceived.

Although all this has always been part of the continuing struggle in America — a struggle between old world evils and the faith and purpose of the American Revolution — it is really un-American: or even anti-American as the founding principles and the great traditions define Americanism. If there are those who think it compatible with loyalty — let alone definitive of it — they have forgotten their American inheritance. And it is dangerous to forget. Let them remember Guizot's question to James Russell Lowell: "How long do you think the American Republic will endure?" and Lowell's famous answer: "So long as the ideas of its founders continue to be dominant."

If then, there must be vows of loyalty, let us choose Lincoln's: "Many free countries have lost their liberties, and ours may lose hers; but if she shall, be it my proudest plume, not that I was the last to desert, but that I never deserted her."

[32] Chapter 9.

15. The Great Evasion

There was once an apprentice clock-maker who found the building of reliable time-pieces too vexing to his patience. So he made a clock out of straw. When, after many futile efforts, this clumsy instrument at last was made to go, it ran for nearly seventeen minutes, then crackled to a stop, worn out. Everyone thought that this was quite remarkable and it brought the young man wide applause. Nevertheless, when the commotion died down, he saw that all that he had was a bundle of straw.

We, in America, are inviting a similar situation. Like the reluctant clock-maker we are apprenticed to a difficult occupation. We are world leaders, without being trained for it and less by choice than force of circumstance. We are required to build something that we are disinclined to build. It demands skills and disciplines to which we are unaccustomed. Fitting together the intricate wheels of world security, each of them meshed with innumerable others, would be a difficult business even under favorable conditions and is much more so when we must undertake it in the presence of a determined enemy who is bent on thwarting us. So, from time to time, we turn away. We would rather build something easier, even though it be made of straw.

It is not that we have done nothing at all that is substantial. The Marshall Plan, for instance, has been rightly

called one of the most enlightened acts of statesmanship
that history records. The same is true of the promise set
forth in 1949 by what we came to call Point Four. In part,
but in very insufficient part, this promise has found embodiment. It is probably true that, apart from the mistake
of immediate demobilization at the end of the war, in the
first years of the aftermath we were doing fairly well; we
were getting a firmer grasp on what was wanted in ideas
and programs.

We had come rather newly to the demands of leadership,
and we had come to them at a very difficult moment. But
we had turned at last towards realities. We knew that we
were facing the dominant fact of the twentieth century,
namely, that the earth's entire population had become a
single vast community. We were living, we told ourselves,
in " one world." In the past, when oceans or natural land
barriers effectually divided one part of the earth from another, a considerable number of communities, some of
them loosely grouped together, lived largely unrelated lives.
One civilization might affect others for a time, through
gradual penetration or invasion, but the rest of the world,
both civilized and otherwise, was very little influenced by
these transitions. With the rise of modern civilization in
the West, however, these limitations were removed, and,
with amazing swiftness, it became apparent that the world
was one community. This we were finally able to perceive.
By the end of the Second World War it was inescapable.
The population of the entire earth was bound together in
a common fate.

It had all happened, especially the final stages, in ways
that exposed us to unmeasured dangers. The ancient way
of things had been disrupted. Much of the world was

devastated. Still more of it was in a ferment. It was a world of revolution. Spiritually and politically, there was widespread confusion. And precisely at the moment when these conditions clamorously revealed themselves and cried out for a remedy, the atomic threat to civilized survival had emerged.

Nor was this all. The miseries of the world were being exploited by the ruthless aims of Communist imperialism. Masquerading as democracy, a movement was spreading through the earth, mobilizing widespread discontent for the very purpose of destroying democracy. We saw this and we said that it was something we must meet. We must meet it militarily; we must meet it politically; we must meet it spiritually. And for a time, we tried to meet it. We knew that we could only do so at great cost; but we also knew — for a little while — that not to meet it was to invite our own doom. Where we failed to lead, the Communists would move in, taking over by default. They would also compete with us even where we *did* intend to lead. It was a strenuous situation.

The majority doubtless saw it less as idealists than as reluctant realists. Just as you cannot have one prosperous family in a township where every other family is destitute and expect that nothing violent will happen, so you cannot have one prosperous nation in a world the rest of which is wretched and hope that there can be security. This was the demand upon us: that we lead in making the entire world a safe place to live in. For if it was not safe for all, it was not safe for any, and so the demand was inescapable. This, as I say, we had begun to see, and were planning to do something about it.

Then something happened — it is hard to say just when

it began: perhaps with the fall of China to the Communists — and we became deflected and divided. It suddenly seemed that we had decided to fight Communism, not by competing with it and resisting it abroad, but by looking for all the people who had ever shaken hands with a Communist in America. The war in Korea, where Communism was really being fought — and bitterly — began to be criticized as though the policy of fighting such a war were itself tinged with Communism. The attempt to expand Point Four so that it was really big enough for the job of putting Communist agitators out of business in the world's most backward and most wretched areas was stubbornly frustrated. The effort to develop ideas with which to defeat the Communist ideas, and to form plans that would draw the world together and make it a safe place to live in, was set aside for political investigations and witchhunts. As I have said, we began to build with straw, and we are still building with straw. The question now is, will it occur to the Communists that straw is an easy thing to set fire to?

In instance after instance, the thought and energy that should have gone into the really urgent problem, the problem of world security under conditions of new and frightening perils, has been put into a series of petty escapisms. We even had a Congressional committee that investigated comic strips. One after another, committees of legislators went forth to seek political fortune by pretending to the American people that their salvation lay in the vivisection of Communist "fronts" and the exhumation of fellow-travellers.

Or, to change the metaphor, it was as though we were out on the ocean, in a leaking ship and with a tornado fol-

lowing, and someone should say, "Now is the time to go
down into the mess-room and hunt for cockroaches." And
the question is, How can we defeat the Communists with
legislators whose mentality is that of cockroach exter-
minators?

It is a dreadful thing that has been happening to us in
these years of the great evasion. Instead of being united
in the effort to understand our situation — which in itself
is no small thing, for comprehension of so changed a
world is very difficult — and equally united in the determination to find a spelled-out policy and program, we are
bitterly divided on issues of inferior importance. We pre-
fer building with straw — and when that grows tedious,
we turn to catching cockroaches.

We have seemed unable to recognize that the Communists are not *making* revolutions, but exploiting them. The
whole of the East is revolutionary. So, in its different way,
is much of the West. People who have never known
hope before have decided that there *is* hope — hope for
them just as much as for Americans. If to turn this hope
into promise they have to raise havoc with their own countries and with the world, they will raise it. There is no
way back. The world of ancient evil is dying. The new
world that is emerging will be ruled by new evils — new
and much worse — unless it is shaped by democracy to
peace and freedom. In other words, unless we take the
American Revolution to these parts of the world, the Russian Revolution will absorb them.

Once again, we have failed to understand our own history. It was *our* revolution, the revolution of liberty and
of the rights of man, that moved the backward populations
to new hope. We had said that all men — not just all

Americans — were created free and equal. Our democracy was not for ourselves alone but, in Lincoln's words, "for man's vast future."

But we are in retreat from the founding principles and have run away from our opportunities. We have left the field to the Communists. Even where we were still holding on — and scoring some successes — we perversely turned them into failures.

There was, for instance, the case of Gordon Ewing, U. S. Foreign Service Officer and Political Program Director of RIAS, the American broadcasting station in Berlin. In the mid-afternoon of June 16, 1953, Mr. Ewing was doing some routine work when the astounding news came through that workers in the Soviet sector were marching on the Communist government buildings.

For most of two days, Mr. Ewing had to make decisions, one after another, of the gravest import and with no margin for error. The station was operated by the United States government. Any broadcast that could be construed by the Russians as an incitement to rebellion might be the pretext for a Soviet attack on West Berlin. On the other hand, the East Germans, revolting against Communist despotism, could not be left without encouragement.

When a workers' delegation from the Soviet sector requested permission to broadcast an appeal for a general strike, Mr. Ewing knew that if the request were granted, the Soviet authorities could not only validly protest, but might claim the right to take precautions lest it happen again. This meant they might have occupied the radio station — and all of Berlin. But he also knew the value to the West of extending the rebellion.

So he merely included a report of the visit of the strike

leaders — and of their plan to strike — on his hourly broadcast, which was just as effective and entirely permissible! Again and again in succeeding hours, he made similar shrewd decisions, and the rebellion grew with every broadcast. Yet, he made no mistakes.

Mr. Ewing deserved decoration. Instead, on the wire service reports he read that he had been named as one of Senator McCarthy's "pro-Communists," the next, apparently, on the list of able and patriotic members of the Foreign Service to be "liquidated."

Writing from Berlin, Stewart Alsop, from whom I take this story, reported that someone whom Mr. Ewing had dismissed because his ability was inadequate to the requirements of his work — RIAS is a highly sensitive outpost of American diplomacy — had been "pouring poison into eagerly receptive American ears." Any disgruntled foreigner, says Mr. Alsop, well knows that he will be well received if he can do anything to "blacken the reputation" of American officials.[33]

Even more destructive in the struggle of American diplomacy to defeat the Communist conspiracy was the "investigation," harrassment and eventual resignation of Theodore Kaghan. This, too, was an achievement of Senator McCarthy's.[34] In the United States, such dismissals have caused but little stir — which is the alarming thing that has been happening to us: we take folly and injustice for granted — but in Germany, as indeed in all Europe, there was deep shock. This, they said to one another, is exactly the sort of thing that happened in the days of Hitler.

[33] See the Stewart Alsop syndicated column, "Matter of Fact," July 20, 1953.
[34] See full and factual account in *The Reporter*, July 21, 1953.

If they needed confirmation for their fears, they soon had it in the almost incredible "book-burning" episode, during which, at one time, there was even doubt whether books by the Secretary of State himself were not being excluded from American overseas libraries.

In the United States, a few thoughtful people may have heard the voice of Luther Evans, Librarian of Congress, who had testified:

"People are deeply moved by what they experience, and I suspect the actuality of free open-handed American libraries overseas means as much to their users as the books they read in them. They may have read about freedom of opinion in the U.S. They actually see evidence of it in our American library that contains books different from or even hostile to the views of the Administration in power in the U.S. The presence of an uncensored book critical of some aspect of American life in the open collections of a U.S. library can do more than a thousand propaganda tracts to convince the doubting reader of the integrity of American goals and the candor with which American shortcomings are admitted." [35]

But Mr. Evans' voice was not heard abroad. There they saw the same purging of ideas that had occurred during Hitler's rise to power. They saw the United States as a country terrified of Communism, its government so fearful of the potency of the Communist appeal that it did not dare to let a Communist book be read.

Indeed, it was worse than that. The third directive from the State Department had ordered publishers to certify that no material sent abroad under a State Department program would be by "Communists, fellow-travellers, or

[35] See the *New Republic*, June 29, 1953, p. 8.

persons who might be controversial." [36]   This directive was withdrawn on the demand of the publishers concerned.

The retreat from the founding principles had now become a rout.   How strangely the words of Jefferson sounded — to the few who remembered: " If the book be false in its facts, disprove them; if false in its reasoning, refute it.   But at all events let us freely hear both sides."

If there is more we might have done to defeat our cause, it is difficult to imagine what it could have been.

Senate committees, before confirming Ambassadors and delegates, have first very largely discredited them, thus reducing as much as possible the dignity and usefulness of their representation.

At the time of the death of Stalin, our diplomacy was half-paralyzed precisely when it should have been most vigorous; even our Ambassador to Russia was detained in America while committees squabbled over his confirmation.

The tour of Messrs. Cohn and Schine in Europe, on behalf of the McCarthy Committee, reduced American diplomacy to caricature and low comedy, and raised questions in Europe of American sanity.

The use of foreign informers to spy on our official representatives has damaged our Foreign Service and undermined respect for the United States itself in the countries where the practice is reported.

Through what they have witnessed, Foreign Service officers have become afraid, in some cases, to report facts to their own State Department, lest through some turn in

---

[36] (Italics added).   My own books were at one time reported banned. Since they are vigorously anti-Communist I must suppose that it was because I had criticized the Congressional committees and was therefore counted " controversial."

events or change in policy, a Congressional committee should attempt to pin guilt upon them by charging that they were sympathetic with what they had reported.

At a time when it is vital to know the facts of world Communism, and to become skilled in their interpretation, the entire research and intelligence branch of the State Department studying Communism in Russia and Asia was eliminated.

The "Voice of America" is all but silent, and even though it speak, who now will hear it?

This, then, is what we owe to those who have sacrificed the solemn obligations of our leadership to their own lust for power, their urge to persecute. And this is what we owe to our own evasion. Even our successes have been largely blighted, and the esteem in which at one time we were widely held is almost gone.

What is the cause of failure? Lack of knowledge? Lack of skill? No, it is a *moral* failure, a *spiritual* defeat. It was never the difficulty of making plans that frustrated us; we are a nation accustomed to complicated undertakings: when we want to do a thing, we do it. It was the will that was lacking — the will, yes, and the vision. We took the wrong things to our hearts.

"Where there is no vision," says the Old Testament, "the people perish." In the last few years, here in America, the vision of the people has been blurred. Perhaps they have wanted it that way. But I doubt that they have wanted the low aims and murky purposes that have taken the place of genuine vision. In any case, the Old Testament is surely right. "Where there is no vision, the people perish."

I would like to believe that very soon all this is going to

change. Unless it does we shall not escape the penalties.
Neither God nor history ever has or ever will suspend the
laws of cause and effect. *And the moral laws are laws of
cause and effect.* They are also laws of ruthless and relentless realism. They have to be. Otherwise, there would be
no reality in the war of right with wrong. And so I say, I
hope there will be a change.

After all, ours is the greatest inheritance ever given to
any nation. If we are willing to exalt it and live up to it,
we have a revolutionary force to let loose upon the world
which would not only defeat Communism but would utterly rout it. If the world should ever come to believe
that we mean to carry liberation to all peoples — liberation
from oppression, from poverty, from centuries of weary and
despairing destitution — by renewing the force and fervor of
our own American Revolution, there is no propaganda that
the Kremlin could devise that would have the slightest
chance of turning the world away from us. *There never
was a propaganda, and there never will be, that can prevail
against the truth men see before their eyes.*

PART FOUR

IN THE TIME REMAINING

16. Between Good and Evil

Whenever we are reminded that human society has become deeply divided, we think first of the antagonism between the western democracies and the countries behind the "iron curtain." The "one world" which was promised has become impossible because the Communists have persisted in frustrating it. This, however, though true as far as it goes, is a very incomplete perception. It leaves out of account, for instance, the very considerable question of how united the world would have become if the Communists had proved co-operative. What we fail to see, except for brief and insufficient intervals, is the division in human society on our own side of the "iron curtain" and the extent to which it is crippling us.

I am not speaking of a division which sets some of us on one side and the rest of us on the other in the various public issues which confront us, though in some respects it does have that effect. I have in mind the conflict of aims and ends which is found not only in the life of our society as a whole but also in the lives of individuals. This is the dividedness that most of all we need to understand: the war within ourselves, the antagonism between good and evil which has produced a deep and painful cleavage in modern culture.

It is this condition of spiritual and moral crisis that is the underlying cause of our dissensions. People who feel —

and who cannot prevent themselves from feeling — the guilt of having rejected the good, and who want to go on rejecting it, grasp anxiously for whatever seems to justify their course. They feel reproached, for instance, by those among their fellow-citizens who have higher aims than their own, and whose concern for the welfare of others has led them into social causes devoted to the common good. Hence, when it became possible to accuse these unselfish people of having sometimes been associated with Communists — no matter how innocent the association actually was — the opportunity was swiftly seized. If the honest aims of good people could be linked with the evil of Communism, then those who felt reproached by these aims could feel less guilty. Or, at any rate, they hoped so.

The Congressional committeeman, looking down from the dais at the nervous and embarrassed witness, feels reinforced in his narrow social outlook when he is able to show that a man of good conscience and generous purpose was " taken in " by the Communists who persuaded him to join a " front " organization. He, the Congressman, was so much " wiser."

So he tries to think. But in the dark recesses of his soul the truth is goading him. To alleviate the pain in his conscience, he browbeats the witness. Like St. Paul on the road to Damascus, he is inwardly persuaded of the goodness of what he hates, and so resists it more intensely.

And in a thousand other ways the people of the modern age, at all levels and in every manner of pursuit, are engaged in this inner struggle which has produced so deep a cleavage in their culture.

We must recognize, of course, that the cleavage is not solely modern: human nature has always been an area of conflict. This is because whatever is human in it must oppose itself to whatever is less than human — to the nature, that is, which it inherits from the animal world. This is possible only in a human society. A man alone (if we could imagine it) would have the shape of a man and perhaps the dawning intelligence of a man, but no mentality, no language, no use of reason, no morality, nothing but a rudimentary spiritual nature, and in fact, no human nature at all except as a potentiality. We become human because we are members of a society which imparts to us its customs, its language, its traditions, its restraints, its aims and purposes — in short, its culture. But we also remain animal. Our animal selves, not only in bone and flesh but in instinct and impulse continue with us. And thus, we cannot escape the conflict.

It is not that the culture imparted to us remains separate and alien and cannot be absorbed into the entirety of us. It *is* absorbed. It makes us what we are — human and unable to be anything less; but also human and unable to leave our animal selves behind. Here we must be careful not to make the mistake that has so often been made and equate the animal with the body and the human with the mind or soul. It is not our animal flesh and blood that we have to contend with but our animal impulses at the human level, our animal callousness and cruelty, our animal urge for dominance, our animal nature conquering our human nature and compelling its resources to serve our animal aims.

Stated in its simplest terms — actually an oversimplification, but so long as we know it is that, a useful one — the overall aim of the animal world is to eat without being eaten. I am aware, of course, that animal nature is more complicated than that, but it is seldom if ever, I think, inconsistent with it. And stated in its simplest terms, that is what animal nature seeks at the human level. In the transition, however, the word "eat" achieves a wider meaning. The hunger of a human being is not merely for food to digest but for worlds to devour. If his animal nature is dominant, his appetite impels him to fatten his ambition for wealth, for power, for fame, for pleasure, for importance — for whatever it is he wants — at the expense of whoever and whatever may stand in his way. He does not physically devour his victims but he devours their welfare and their happiness. He believes that unless he does this, his own welfare and happiness will be devoured. This he does as a business man, a member of a profession, a politician, a diplomatist, a trade union leader, or even as an obscure employee anxious to "get ahead." The only difference between such a person and a lower animal attempting to eat without being eaten is that the human pattern is more elaborate. It is with this, then, that human nature must contend in trying to subdue the animal and make the human dominant. This is the essence of the conflict. This it is that keeps us inwardly divided.

But as I have said, the conflict is not new. It began with the beginning of human society. Little by little, man the animal, with the human potentiality stirring within him, built up traditions and restraints, and out of the inner mystery of his being came reinforcement for them through the growth of conscience. Gradually, by a development just as real as the one which had formed him physically, giving him his distinctive brain and upright posture, he arrived at concepts of justice and righteousness, and discovered the possibility of sympathy and kindness, and presently in the culture of his society these concepts and possibilities became commanding. Prophets arose to tell him he must "do justly and love mercy," and his human nature, no matter how he rebelled against such difficult requirements, confirmed that what the prophets said was true. He himself wanted justice; he himself needed mercy. What he asked of others, he must also ask of himself. His reasoning mind stood with his conscience. This was the nature of reality — of his own reality and of the mystery from which it came. This was the behest of the ultimate, this was the commandment of God.

How it happened in detail, through the slow movement of the centuries, is of course the entire story of religion — indeed, it is the central theme in the whole history of man. Yet, no matter how often the story is repeated, we fail to keep in view its full significance. We think that spiritual evolution is less real, less conclusive than physical evolution; though the truth is that the emergence of the moral and spiritual is in all respects a part of the natural evolution of life. Unless we are to say that man himself is unnatural, we must include him with all he is and does within the world of nature. The fact that his morality — like his creative mind and his esthetic sense and his spirituality — comes to him as a member of a society does not make it less real or less a part of the evolutionary process than is the case when a parent bird teaches its young to fly. It is not necessary to appeal to theology, or to subscribe to dogmas to see that man is a spiritual, moral being, whose human nature is as natural as his animal nature. And the two are at war within him. That is why there is so much guilt in the world, so much frustration, and so little confidence, so little peace of mind.

This, then, is the background of the matter. If we have understood it, we shall see more clearly why the struggle between good and evil has produced a cleavage in our modern culture. For we do not belong to a primitive society. We belong to a civilization the culture of which has been powerfully affected by the Judeo-Christian tradition. The great pleas for righteousness by the prophets of the Old Testament are sacred to us and the life of Jesus of Nazareth is a vital part of our inheritance. We affirm the principles that Jesus taught. "Do unto others as ye would that they should do unto you." The moral and spiritual development within our culture has reached a high point. It is essential to our spiritual sustenance. We cannot renounce it; but we do not live in accordance with it. Hence the cleavage.

What was once a conflict the outcome of which was postponable, and which we neither won nor lost but just continued with, has become, in the changed state of the world, a conflict that must have an issue. Something must soon be settled. Indeed, the entire question must be settled. Because, as the world now stands, people divided within themselves, and forming a society equally divided, cannot expect to endure. Their civilization will not long survive the cleavage in their culture.

How deep that cleavage is can be illustrated — if illustration is necessary — by remembering that to a growing child in a normal home the mother stands for love and compassion, gentleness and unselfishness. She teaches her children that these are the virtues that they most of all must try to acquire. She appeals to the Bible and to the ethical precepts of the Judeo-Christian religion. Or she tells the story of moral exemplars of the Christian centuries, or of brave

and unselfish men and women among the national heroes
of her own country. In any case, what she stands for is
love and generosity, kindness and forbearance, and " doing
unto others as ye would that they should do unto you."

When her children attend the church school, they hear
the same precepts. They are encouraged to act accord-
ingly. Their growing humanity is molded by the best and
noblest in our culture. It becomes a part of what they
are — a part, but unhappily not all.

For meanwhile, they have been learning other lessons.
Harsh rivalries and even cruelties are readily condoned if
they fit into certain categories. The newspaper that father
reads — or even mother, for that matter, for she, too, is a
divided person — results in a quite different attitude from
that derived from Scriptural sources. You are supposed to
" love your neighbor as yourself " but not if he is colored.
You are supposed to condemn lies but not if they are help-
ful to your politics. You are supposed to have compassion
for the destitute but not if it costs money. As for doing
unto others as ye would that they should do unto you, this
is qualified by the need to " get ahead." Jesus was a great
person, and he said some fine things, but it's best not to
take him too seriously — which you don't, after a while;
you just use his name to swear with.

The cleavage begins, as is now evident, when we are
quite young; which is one reason, perhaps, why so many
adult Americans are afflicted with what the psychologists
call " Momism." It is not the only reason, of course, but it
is certain that American men of all ages, while engaged
in the harsh and competitive business of " getting ahead "
are inwardly troubled by their memory of the kind and
gentle world their mothers represented to them. Except

for a hardened few, there is no way of wholly forgetting that world of hopes and dreams.

The same is true of the world that was promised at the inception of American democracy. Those great principles live in our hearts and the fact is that we love them. " Liberty and justice for all " — the words are spoken by our school children day after day and who can doubt that they have impact? When, therefore, we see liberty encroached upon and justice transgressed and the great decencies of American life derided and trampled, we become sharply aware of the cleavage.

From personal life to foreign policy, from the individual alone to the world in its entirety, we are divided — inwardly and painfully divided. The struggle between good and evil has become climactic and must have an issue. Divided people cannot make a united society — and a divided society cannot survive. We have tried to hide this from ourselves, and for a long time, to one extent or another, we have succeeded. But it cannot continue. As John Steinbeck has put it in a recent novel: " . . . there is one story in the world, and only one, that has frightened and inspired us. . . . Humans are caught — in their lives, in their thoughts, in their hunger and ambitions, in their avarice and cruelty, and in their kindness and generosity, too — in a net of good and evil. . . . Virtue and vice were the warp and woof of our first consciousness, and they will be the fabric of our last. . . . There is no other story. . . . All novels all poetry, are built on the never-ending contest in ourselves of good and evil." [1]

This is the contest, when evil is winning, that makes Communists, and also tyrants and oppressors who are not

[1] John Steinbeck, *East of Eden* (N.Y.: Viking Press, 1952), p. 413.

Communists. This, as we have seen earlier, from a somewhat different starting-point, is what makes persecutors — and the applauders of persecutors.

But the struggle cannot now continue without decisive victories. One way or the other, there must be victories. Justice and righteousness, compassion and sympathy, love and benevolence — these human and humane endowments must come at last and claim their own. Or if we will not have it so, then what we are without them will destroy us. We have seen several times within our own lifetimes that out of this cleavage and because we would not end it, there has sprung upon the world a brutality unprecedented in the Christian era. The animal nature, seizing dominance, has used the material forces of our civilization to bring it close to dissolution.

And there the question stands. There is only one issue. We are moral and spiritual not by choice and not by accident; we are moral and spiritual by necessity. We became so in becoming human. It was intended. God made us so. It is our torment and could be our glory. That also was intended. In the poetry of the ancient words, "He breathed into man's nostrils the breath of life, and man became a living soul."

17. The Neglected Dimension

I was asked not long since, concerning a friend of mine, as to whether his thinking was not rather leftish. This gave me an opportunity that I had been wanting for some time. " I am not sure that I understand the question," I replied. " What do you mean by leftish? Leftish of what? " " Oh, you know what I mean," my interrogator countered. " Leftish in his ideas, not Communist or anything like that, but a good deal left of center." " Well," I said, " I do know that he's not Communist, but I can't tell you whether he's left of center because I don't know where the center is. Center of what? " Whereupon my questioner began to show a little irritation, for which, secretly, I did not blame him, for he was using phrases with which he knew I must be quite familiar, and I seemed to him to be quibbling in an effort to avoid a straightforward answer.

But I was not quibbling. I was merely demonstrating, as much for my own benefit as anybody else's, that this familiar jargon about left and right is very indefinite in its meaning. We are told, for instance, that it is very leftish to believe in public ownership of economic facilities, such as means of transportation and communication. Yet, highways are means of transportation, and the postal system is a means of communication, and both are publicly owned, presumably with the approval of people who are

sure that they are not leftish. If you travel on rails, however, instead of concrete, you move to the left of center if
you think that the government should take them over.
The same thing is said of you if you believe that fast communication as well as the slow kind — namely the telephone system in addition to letter-carrying — should pass
to public ownership. I am not implying, of course — and
I suppose I should make that clear — that I am myself in
favor of these proposals: I think it better that the railroads
and the telephone systems remain under their present
management. But if anyone says that this places me somewhere to the right of center, I deny it. It merely makes
known what I think about the ownership of railroads and
telephone systems within the United States of America.
If I happened to be visiting England, I would be quite
content to have the telephone system operated by the government — as it has been almost since the beginning — but
I might be rather sorry about the government operation of
the railroads. If I am told that this means that in America
I am somewhat to the right of center and as a visitor to England slightly to the left, I reply that such chatter is meaningless. Left and right have nothing to do with the matter;
the only thing that is central is my wish to hold intelligent
opinions.

How vacant of meaning this unthinking jargon eventually becomes is made completely evident when we consider that Communism is supposed to be to the extreme
left and yet tyranny is supposed to be reactionary, and thus
to the extreme right. Communist tyranny is therefore both
right and left, and as far away from itself as possible in both
directions. Which is manifestly nonsense. What we
should say of Communism is not that it is to the *left* but

that it is lower — lower than democracy — and thus we might begin to have some vertical distinctions.

And that is what I told the man who inquired about my friend's thinking — as to whether it was leftish. Why should a man's thinking have only two dimensions — and even those confused ones? My friend's thinking, I said, is the product of a fine mind and therefore much too elaborate to be imprisoned within a foolish metaphor. His opinions on some matters are more or less conservative: that is, he supports existing arrangements and wants them to continue; on other matters, he desires changes and can tell you why he thinks they would be for the better. But in all matters, he tries to think honestly and to arrive at opinions which are not weighted with bias or distorted by prejudice. And therefore, if he is to be described by any sort of lineal metaphor, it had better be by a perpendicular one. His thinking has stature and he, himself, is upright.

How strange it is that this third and indispensable dimension has been so much lost sight of in a country of tall buildings and in an age of aviation where there is so much encouragement to look upwards and to measure ourselves not only by the length and breadth of the earth's surface but by the distance between earth and sky. Moreover, since our tall buildings have taught us that height must be based upon depth, and that the farther up you go, the deeper you must dig to give an edifice secure foundations, how is it that we remain addicted to the shallow?

It seems at times that shallowness is almost a cult. If anyone says anything that indicates that he takes pains to think carefully, and especially if he says it in precise language which conveys exactly what he means, he is regarded with suspicion. All sorts of silly ways are found to make him seem an oddity, and this is done, of course, because those who do it are afraid of him; he has a third dimension — depth and height — and life seems safer — or at least easier — if it goes a-crawling on the ground.

What a pity it all is! Our public life needs elevation. What is there that can rescue us from the partisan spirit and take our earth-bound, horizontal aims and give them altitude? Some of us have become tired of hearing about right and left; we want to hear about right and wrong. When we are told, for instance, that to work for better race relations is leftish, our reply must be that those who say so have lost their vertical dimensions and have sunk below the level of their conscience. It is not a left and right distinction; it is a right and wrong distinction.

So it is with a great many other matters. The issues before us require us to choose between good and evil and to put before all other loyalties the loyalty to conscience. To see the questions that this generation must settle as matters of conflict between an amorphous left and a shapeless right — or merely as a struggle between political parties and their factions — as though no other and more decisive factor were involved, is to see them obscurely and falsely.

What we must see is that a clamant need exists to find the truth in all these issues and declare it plainly; to discover the just purpose and the righteous aim and to follow where conscience leads us. We must recover the lost dimension — the vertical dimension of depth in our attachment to what is right and of height in moral stature. No loyalty to parties, churches, movements, institutions or anything else whatever must keep us shrunken or enslaved in partisan allegiance. We must be free people, with free minds, thinking honestly, speaking sincerely, resolving righteously, and not afraid to stand up, tall enough in righteous principle to see the evils in the world about us — and rebuke them. It is not what we do about left and right that will save us, but what we do about right and wrong.

18. The Cultivation of Kindness

The callousness and cruelty of which persecution is an outcome can be attributed to malice, and usually correctly. But malice does not come from nowhere. Its emotional sources must be sought in impulses which at one time might have taken a better direction. Is it then possible that if we understood more about kindness — the opposite alternative to callousness and cruelty — we might be able, by actual choice and cultivation, to achieve a healthier emotional condition?

Certainly, the urge to persecute, although it can be restrained by law, cannot be really mastered except morally and spiritually. And since, in emotional life, evil motives can only be expelled by good ones that replace them, it seems necessary that we should ask, not only what public measures should be taken for the suppression of persecution, but what might be done in personal lives to increase comprehension and kindness.

Much might be done, it is true, merely by returning to the wholesome austerities of justice. But even to do this — to create the will to do it — requires a change of moral attitude. This brings us once again to the emphasis with which we started: the emphasis upon *people*.

It can scarcely be doubted — though, of course, it cannot actually be demonstrated — that there is less kindness in the world today than there used to be. The brutality of two world wars and the coarsening effect of the aftermath have taken their toll of the gentler virtues. So have the new oppressions and tyrannies. Even in countries like our own which have suffered comparatively little from the direct effects of war and which have not yet been trampled under the heels of tyrants, there are stridencies and tensions which make people less likely to be kind than harsh. Kindness comes most easily when people are happy and content. If they are insecure and fearful, they are prone to feel resentment and hostility, and this makes all friendly qualities more difficult to maintain.

That, I believe, is our situation at the present time. The difficult phase into which mankind has entered, so fraught with peril and beset with uncertainty, is having its effect upon individual lives. So is the loss of firm belief and the feeling that life has direction and should be meaningful. People who have lost their bearings and who do not think that anything in the long run is dependable can readily become islands of brooding discontentment, cut off from sympathy with their fellow-mortals. To such people, kindness at best is only a gesture; they do not *feel* it, there is nothing within them that generates it.

This is not the *necessary* effect of disillusion or disinheritance; but it is a probable effect, and perhaps a prevailing one. It means that people stop being kind when fortune ceases to smile upon them. The question might be raised, however, as to whether there was much depth in this sort of kindness even when it was plentiful. It was just a sort of overflow from a contented mood, a bonus to the world out of a personal superabundance. The poet, Alexander Pope, seems to have had this in mind when he wrote:

"Who does a kindness is not therefore kind;
　Perhaps prosperity becalm'd his breast;
　Perhaps the wind just shifted from the East."

Or, in short, because things were going well with him, he had no reason to feel ill-disposed towards other people. He could afford generosity; he had time for what would pass for sympathy.

But was this ever kindness? There is a proverb which says that "kindness is a language the deaf can hear and the dumb can understand." This means, I take it, that its genuineness is unmistakable and that no one can be in doubt, not even a person of impaired perceptions, when the true quality of kindness is being manifested. Does this require that kindness can never be achieved by deliberate decision: that it always must be spontaneous?

This is, I know, to many people, a very torturing question. When they come to some of us for counsel, they complain that they are unable to feel towards other people — even towards their families and their friends — as they would like to feel. They are hostile or cold, irritable and unsympathetic — which is not at all the way they want to be; but if they act differently than they feel, if they speak friendly words and do kindly deeds, they fear that they are hypocrites.

They want at least to be candid with themselves — and, to the extent they find possible, candid with other people. And of course, candor is a good thing. But if candor is a solitary virtue, unaccompanied by other qualities, it does not get us very far. It is all very well for people to analyze themselves honestly, but if they are going to leave themselves where they found themselves there is not much gain in it. It is like putting a child with a dirty face in front of a mirror; you want him not only to see the dirt but to turn his thoughts to soap and water. Yes, and you want him to wash his face even if he doesn't feel like it. When he has washed his face often enough and accepted it as a civilized custom you hope that he *will* feel like it. You have not turned him into a hypocrite because you have introduced him to soap and water when he didn't feel friendly to soap and water: all you have done is turn a lazy boy with a dirty face into an occupied boy with a clean one.

The truth about many people who are afraid that if they tried to be kind it would be hypocritical is uncomfortably similar. They are emotionally lazy. They would rather accept themselves with their indolent habit of not feeling friendly than occupy themselves with thoughts and deeds which would teach them to be friendly. Kindness, at the beginning, is quite often not spontaneous; it has to be cultivated. Children are not born kind; they may have what the psychologists call empathy but it takes a good deal of practice before they achieve sympathy. There is such a thing as an " educated heart." Indeed, emotion must always be educated and it always is. The trouble is that sometimes it is very badly educated, or under-educated, or — to use again the language of the psychologist — it is badly conditioned.

Let us consider the meaning of the word *kindness*. It comes from a root-word of Gothic and Teutonic origin, the word *kin*. Kindness originally is the sort of behavior that should be shown to one's family, one's kin. The Latin equivalent would be *gen*, from which we have the word, *generosity,* which means acting towards people outside one's family as one should act to those within it. But the word goes still further back. *Kin* in the Gothic, *gen* in the Latin, *gen* also in the Greek, and *jan* in the Sanscrit all mean the bearing or producing of children. It is therefore to the mother that the word finally refers and kindness most literally is the way a mother behaves towards her children, and then, by reflection, the way the children behave towards her. This behavior, by gradual extension, comes to include the other members of the family, and then, friends and neighbors; those outside.

We can see at once, therefore, that there is a learning process, even though originally it was confined chiefly to the home. Indeed, we can say even now that kindness is chiefly learned in the home — or, and this is the sad fact we have to face, by *not* being learned in the home it has not been learned at all. Parents who do not teach their children kindness — and by example — do them as much injury as though they had maimed their bodies or undermined their health. Again and again, those of us to whom people come for counsel discover that most of these people were unfortunate in their parents, and if it is kindness or love that they cannot achieve, the reason for it can be traced back to their homes.

Nevertheless, they can still learn kindness if they are willing for it: if they will stop telling themselves that if they are other than hostile to people, or callous, they are hypocrites. Behavior patterns really can be changed by practice. And such efforts are not hypocritical unless we insist upon remaining prisoners of a lazy insincerity.

Let us at least reach this starting-point: kindness can be cultivated; in fact, it *must* be cultivated; it always *is* cultivated. If it has not been cultivated in childhood so that it has become natural in the young adult, it can be cultivated whenever we decide upon it, and a *little* success is possible even in advanced old age. I am not saying that Ebenezer Scrooge in Dickens' *Christmas Carol* would make a representative case history. In real life he would probably not have given Bob Cratchitt a turkey for Christmas dinner and a raise in salary, but he would have given him a jar of cranberry jelly and perhaps have mellowed a bit in his opposition to social security. This, however, is the extreme case. What I wish to emphasize is that it is possible at any time in life to begin the cultivation of kindness.

How do you do it? First of all, by the use you make of imagination. If what you have done with it down to now is chiefly to weave a world of fantasy about yourself, you move out from this world and project yourself into the lives of other people. This is what Jesus asked of the people whom, more than all others, he criticized severely: the Pharisees. Their virtue was cold and lifeless, limited by being self-centered and dull and lacking in insight — limited, in short, because it lacked imagination. Jesus, a highly imaginative person himself, was outraged and impatient at the slowness of these people's comprehension. Their imaginations were too drugged by self-obsession, self-preoccupation: yes, and too lazy, too sluggish. He wanted them to move out into the lives of other people, to see how it felt to belong to a despised class, or what it was that made objectionable people act as they did. He obviously believed that not only poets and geniuses, but quite ordinary people could make much better use of their imagination.

And he was right. Not only in understanding *groups* of people and thereby feeling more kindly towards them, but in very personal relationships we make inadequate use of our imaginations. How *do* we use them? Is it not to make out our own case? Seething with resentment and blinded by bitterness, we build up a picture of the person — or persons — to whom we are antagonistic, which picture is true only to our own morbid emotions, and not in the least true to life. Suppose — it will take an effort but it is worth making — suppose we try to imagine those other persons as they seem to themselves. Suppose we try to feel what they are feeling. In all cases, it should bring us to sanity, and in most cases it could bring us to kindness. Not to a lot of kindness — not at first. But to *some* sympathy — some of the compassion that we should feel for each other since we are all kinfolk in our strange life on the earth, all wounded by battles we have fought and lost, all in need of understanding and friendship. This would at least be a beginning.

But of course, we do not do it even in much easier cases. Here, for example, you are driving (we will suppose) up Georgia Avenue in Washington. In front of you is a car driven by an old lady who seems uncertain until the last minute whether she will go to the right of the little traffic island where people get off the trolley cars, or go straight ahead following the tracks — or perhaps try a little of both. And you wish this stupid creature who should have her license taken away would make up her mind so that you can pass her on one side or the other. So you blow your horn and frighten her nearly to death, and when you pass her you give her a look that almost sets fire to her old-fashioned spring hat, and with a feeling of superiority sustained and virtue vindicated, you pass on your way.

But suppose you had a better trained imagination.

Maybe this old lady is *not* a good driver, but she drives slowly and is not likely to run over anybody. In any case, she *had* to go to the Safeway to do the shopping. And even if she's a poor driver, she's surely a wonderful cook. Moreover, this old lady has lived rather a brave life. Nothing spectacular, but she went through the depression very gallantly when her husband was out of work. She managed pretty well when her sons were overseas, and still does, though one of them has never been the same since his wartime experiences. She is a good mother-in-law, and has more than half persuaded herself that the women her sons have married are worthy of them; and as a grandmother, she is just exactly right. Moreover, she is not unintelligent. Although she claims to know nothing of politics, people of both parties have been known to listen to her in amazement now and then, because of the simple way in which she decides between right and wrong and you can't talk her out of it. Just an ordinary old lady, as I say: nothing outstanding, nothing remarkable. But what sort of person were *you* when a few minutes ago you blew that impatient blast on your horn? Oh, you will do it again, of course. But perhaps you will feel a little foolish afterwards because these paragraphs may have made a contribution — a small but definite contribution — to your emotional education!

Kindness grows with practice. And it begins with training your imagination. Kindness is *not* just doing what you feel like doing — or what you think you feel like doing; certainly not that at the beginning. I say " what you *think* you feel like doing " because at any given time you are likely to feel like doing not just one thing but any of several things: you may feel like doing one thing and at the same time may want to do its opposite. After all, the desire to act decently, if we follow it, carries its own reward. We wish for that reward: self-respect, the sense of being a bit more grown up. So it often happens that we *do* feel like being kind — but the feeling against it may be stronger. In this case, we can decide to be kind, if we will, even though the impulse to do so is not at present the stronger. This is the way to cultivate kindness — and we do cultivate it, just as we cultivate a sense of beauty in the appreciation of art or music, or as we develop a skill through co-ordinating our brain and nerves and muscles until they do easily and naturally what at first they refused to do at all.

This is the *beginning* of the cultivation of kindness. And once begun, no one will need to tell us how to continue. Each step reveals the next. But it takes genuine effort to begin: patience, outgoing thought, imagination, and at the same time — not later — the effort to be kind: just to do as you wish that people would do to you. And gradually, as some of your life flows into the lives of other people and into the life of stricken humanity, you find that sympathy has become natural to you, that other people are your kin, your spiritual family, and belong with you and you with them. This that should have happened in your childhood — or begun to happen — is happening to you in your later years. You become trained in outgoing interest, in consideration for other people, in friendliness and love.

If it be said that in the course of this chapter we have moved somewhat into the direct field of religion — out of the arena of politics, so to speak, and " into church " — the answer is that this is what we need to do. As the manager of a national political campaign once said to me, " We shall get nowhere until we turn the water of politics into the wine of religion."

He did not mean — and nor do I — that the separation of church and state should be abridged. This could only result in a baneful loss for both. But religion is not bounded by churches. Nor is it confined within creeds and transmitted only through rituals. It is, as Lincoln put it, " a spirit in the life." And certainly, wherever it comes, it is the spirit that engenders sympathy and kindness.

So there it is! To the extent that any of us, leaders or ordinary citizens, are willing for the simplicity — and humility — of this approach to the moral crisis of the modern world, we shall be on the way to banishing the stridencies and tensions which have let loose among us the urge to persecute.

19. About Being an American

The claim I have advanced in these pages that the United States as a nation is founded upon moral principles, the betrayal of which it would be impossible to survive, will be contested. Such a view of American history, it will be said, is far too idealistic. Actually, what keeps the country going is a system of checks and balances, all of them related in one way or another to the basic fact of self-interest.

Since, if this contention is true, it weakens our case to the extent that we have appealed to the founding principles, before closing we shall examine it.

The system of checks and balances is said to apply first of all to the various arms of government, ensuring that no one of them — the executive, the legislative, the judicial — exceeds its authority. But it also applies to capital and labor, to producer and consumer, to any one interest as over against all other interests, and so it is supposed that although from time to time there may be trouble — trouble arising because of the attempt of any one of these elements to gain advantage over the rest — nonetheless, the trouble will always soon die down; it will do so because of the checks and balances.

If it be asked what keeps this system going, what makes it automatic and dependable, the answer is self-interest. The self-interest of one — whether an individual or a

group — is counteracted by the self-interest of others. So
that there has to be an adjustment of each to all. And if
in some respect there is an overweighting or some excess, a
little time is certain to correct it.

The question is, then: Is this true? Can self-interest do
what is expected of it? Now, I am not an economist, not
a sociologist, not even a politician. Nevertheless, to this
question I will give a direct answer — history's answer.
Self-interest will *not* do what is expected of it. Actually, it
never did; and there is nothing more certain than that it
never will.

If the people of the United States cannot rise above the
motive of self-interest, those who are saying that our system is near the end of its tether will prove correct. It is
not a matter of chance; it is a thing proved by previous experience. It has happened before.

If Plato could be suddenly resurrected and given a chance
to survey the American scene, he would say, "Just as I
told you! Just as I always said! A democracy must sink
to the level of the lowest; the lowest motive is self-interest.
The greed of each will destroy the good of all. Therefore
your democracy, as I can see, is doomed." Aristotle would
say the same. Indeed, we can quote him. "A democracy,"
he said, "when put to the strain, grows weak, and is supplanted by oligarchy." [2] And of course, the synonym for
oligarchy, in an industrial civilization, is fascism. We can
learn a lot about ourselves if we know a little about fifth
and fourth century Greece.

So can we if we understand the factors which turned the
ancient Roman democracy into an imperial tyranny. Some
of them were economic. Others were the weakness of the

[2] *Rhetoric*, I.

legislature, the impossibility of the Senate — the Roman Senate — making up its mind. The pressure of special interests was a factor; particularly commercial interests. So was demagoguery. But most of all it was frustration. When Augustus deprived the representative department of the Roman government of many of its powers, he did so reluctantly. But if action could not be had in other ways, if all that the legislative processes of government could promise was stalemate and frustration, the executive would have to assume the powers required. Augustus chanced to be a strong executive, but if he had been a weak one he would soon have been supplanted. This is the way it has to work. Exigency provides the need; the need produces the strong man. But the outcome is never — never, that is, for long — a happy one.

What can we do if democracy is based only on self-interest? On that basis, Thomas Carlyle is forever right: " Democracy," he says, " is by the nature of it, a self-cancelling business: and gives in the long run a net result of zero." [3] Even Emerson, in a despondent mood, declared a lack of faith in what he saw as passing for democracy. " Democracy is morose," he said, " and runs to anarchy." [4]

What shall we say of all this testimony? Have we, as some suppose, reached an impasse in American affairs? Is it true that democracy must carry the seeds of its own decay? That under strain it will prove too weak to last?

The answer can be very simple. Democracy will not endure if its basis is self-interest. If we are to depend upon checks and balances, and if that is all we have to depend upon, we are already lost. It may be that in its initial

---

[3] *Chartism*, VI.
[4] " Nominalist & Realist."

phases a democracy can be maintained by the self-interest of each competing with the good of all. I doubt even that, but there are historians who suppose so. If they are right, the fact remains that such democracies do not endure. They cease after they have exhausted the initial phase.

But in our own case, there are unprecedented circumstances: we do not have a classical democracy, or even our own earlier agrarian one; the industrial revolution has issued in all the challenging factors of the machine age; we have a world situation involving very onerous and inescapable responsibilities. No problem is any longer only a local problem, or a national problem: it swiftly becomes a world problem. Self-interest exerting political pressure on Congress can have enormous international impact, encouraging, perhaps, conditions which make for despair and tyranny, and presently for war.

No previous situation, not even ancient Rome's, was quite like ours. If the processes of government within the United States are obstructed and stultified, American influence will at once decline. It is declining now. The result can be extremely tragic. If the United States goes upon the basis of self-interest at home, the United States will also go upon the basis of self-interest abroad. These interests interlock — and this, again, is what is happening. National democracy is only a part of what is involved. International democracy, too — and the hope of its survival — is just as much at stake.

So that it comes to this: the American system cannot be maintained by self-interest at home and it cannot be protected by self-interest abroad. There *must* be an adoption of a higher level.

That is why we must understand better what it means to

be an American. Some among us are ceasing to be Americans; others have *never been* Americans. They are just people who happened to be born here. Let us define the situation further.

From the beginning there has been divergence as to what it means to be American. For some, even of the colonials, it meant a chance to get rich quick, a chance to exploit, a chance to achieve selfish ends without much interference. That is why there was slavery. That is why there were industrial " robber barons." That is why there have been so many grafting political bosses and such a number of corrupt demagogues. " Never give someone you can cheat an even break! If he could cheat *you*, he *would*. Grab all you can! That is America! "

For some, therefore, unbridled materialism has been their attachment to America. Just as a boastful nationalism has; and all the various sorts of exploitation. This is what it has always meant — to some — to be American. And whether they are capitalists, trade union leaders, politicians, or even ordinary citizens, it is this " Americanism " that is threatening our national ruin. They want — these sordid worshippers of power and greed — to stage a battle of self-interests; they want to fight it ruthlessly no matter what the consequence to other people — or to America's place in a broken and despairing world. They are always isolationists, these people; they are national isolationists because they are personal isolationists. The nation and the world exist *for them*.

If anyone presents them with ideals, with humanitarian purposes, they are scornful — except in public. Demagogically, such ideas are sometimes useful, and unfortunately, there is nothing more vulgar, more hypocritical, more thoroughly mean-minded than some of the " patriotic " speeches we hear about being an American. The very word " Americanism " has fallen into disrepute among a lot of decent people. They don't want any of it. But perhaps they concede too much. Perhaps they must redeem the word. In losing the battle of words they may lose the battle of ideas. If they are not careful, they may lose their country.

I, for my part, deny that self-interest is the controlling characteristic of a true American. I deny that jingoism is American. I deny that foolish pride and empty boasts of power and wealth define Americans. All these things are old world evils, carried to a land of larger opportunity. The opportunity being larger, the evils can be worse. But they are not American. They are betrayals of America.

Moreover, I believe that in this nation, democracy never has been workable merely through checks and balances or competitive interests. I believe that there has been — has always been — a concern for justice, a feeling for fair play, an attachment to restraint and reasonableness, a commitment to the common welfare, a humanitarian outlook, a desire to be of help to others — the total range of qualities, in fact, which have recently been called, " good neighborliness."

This, I say, was the distinction of the New World from the beginning — because it was hoped to carry it to a new and universal measure of achievement. It was not freedom alone — the liberty to do what you liked — that America was founded upon. It was unity, too. The largest nation of free people ever known to history was given freedom because it was given unity. No special interest can do this. No sectionalism can do it. What these individuals, these special interests, these sectional groups always desire is to make the whole society serve their will — so that they can take more than their share of what the efforts of the entire nation have provided. That, I say, is not American.

If Washington was a representative American, if Jefferson was such, if Lincoln has defined our national standards, then greed and lust for power are not American.

As Thomas Mann has put it, the "greatest strength [of democracy is] in its deep spiritual and moral self-consciousness." It accepts responsibility. It sees the individual in relation to all his obligations and asks him to rise, of his own accord, to the level of them. Democracy is not a system of checks and balances, except in a secondary way. Democracy is brotherhood in political and social embodiment. In short, democracy is spiritual. It is not a way of government unless it is first a way of life; it is not the form of a society unless it is also the faith of that society.

Therefore, no amount of compulsion can restore a democratic system when it fails. It can only produce another system — a system of compulsion, an *un*democratic system. For democracy depends for its working upon the faith and purpose in the hearts of the people, upon the level of their public interests, upon their vision, their ideals. If it is not in your heart to use restraint, to practice patience, to allow for fair play, then no amount of legislation can put it there. If one section of the country is manipulating advantages at the expense of another; if politicians sell themselves to special interests or demagogic opportunities; if there is nothing but greed and envy everywhere — then democracy cannot endure no matter how many laws are passed.

There *must* be dedication to the common welfare. It

must even surpass a dedication to the national interests of America. I agree with the writers of the *City of Man*, who say that " he who is *only* an American is not yet an American." For the founding principles are universal. The need abroad is just as much an obligation as the need at home. Human rights do not cease at national frontiers, and neither does responsibility. If this did not appear so in the past it was because conditions then did not so obviously proclaim it. Today, the earth — we have heard it over and over again — is just one neighborhood. Fair play is needed not only in one place but in all places; justice is essential everywhere. And more than justice. Mercy! Compassion! And that is part of what it means to be American.

But this is not at all what it means to be American as the super-patriots and the professional anti-Communists define it. They do not see that opposition to Communism must be on moral grounds — and the fact that they do not see it is far from contradicted by their frequent references to " godlessness." What they dislike about Communism, apparently, is not its perversions of the truth, or its corrupted justice, or its tyranny and profanation of the sacredness of human rights — for they are willing to pervert the truth themselves and to be unjust and tyrannous. To gain their ends they are contemptuous of the sacredness of human rights. So much so that in their conduct they resemble Communists. As to what they *do* care for, it seems to be — no matter what the cost — their own advancement. For this they will conspire as stealthily as any commissar. They undermine our true Americanism. They make the struggle harder.

To defeat Communism, we need our spiritual inheritance. These men disdain it. To defeat Communism, we need the unity our Fathers gave us. These men are sowers of dissension. To defeat Communism, we must uphold traditional American principles. These men betray them. To defeat Communism, we must advance democracy. These men reverse its progress. To defeat Communism, we must uphold our moral standards. These men ignore them. To defeat Communism, we must be just and righteous, among ourselves and in the world at large. These men frustrate this aim. To defeat Communism, we must have courage. These men are making cowards of their fellow-citizens. To defeat Communism, we must hold high our faith in freedom. These men are tyrannous. And, finally, to defeat Communism, we must be spiritually superior to it. These men degrade the soul.

If they are not repudiated in the name of true Americanism, they will impose their counterfeit upon us to pave the way for tyranny.

There is no better way of life than the fully and truly American and none with greater freight of promise. There is nothing quite so precious in the world of nations — even now when much is lost. To depart from it is to lose what centuries of slow and painful progress have provided, centuries which go far back beyond the colonizing of these shores; to lose it not only for ourselves, but for the world.

Let me repeat: the American commitment is to universal justice, the rights of all men, not the special interests of some. It is a commitment to fair play, to patience, to tolerance, to neighborliness. It is a commitment to the common good. It protects liberty with unity, the opportunity of each with the good of all. It is compassionate, humanitarian. It believes in man and in his future. It is the Golden Rule, the rule of brotherhood in action. It is based upon the claim of conscience and the faith in goodness. It begins not in a system but within the heart.

It battles prejudice and false opinion: it seeks the truth. It is opposed to barriers of exclusiveness: its principles are universal. It has no place for persecution: its attachment is to human rights. It despises cowardice, including moral cowardice. But it also has no use for obstinacy, inflexibility and intolerance. It prefers honesty to cleverness, kindness to self-sufficiency, good-will to narrow-minded aims. It is a way of life now, and a faith, a vision of the future. It is a purpose to be served.

If anyone asks by what right I define these characteristics as American, I point him once more to those Americans the rest of us revere as great. I say that America is defined by the moral progress she has sought, and by exemplars, not by the hour of perfidy and by her little-minded, greedy men. And if anyone tells me that these characteristics are more than American, that they are universal, I will reply that that is why they are American. Because this nation was *not* founded on the divisive and the exclusive, but upon the rights of all mankind.

Can we restore these standards? Can we seek again the touch of greatness? The future will depend upon the answer.

Hence I am pleading for religion. I have been all along. Not for a special creed. Not for a ritual. Not for a particular church. But for the religion — it really was religion — that first gave to the United States its soul. For the religion of which Tom Paine was so passionate a prophet, and Thomas Jefferson so persistent an expositor and pioneer. For the religion Walt Whitman set to verse, the religion of which Abraham Lincoln is a treasured symbol.

It is a belief in man. And therefore in brotherhood. A belief in all the decencies of life that flow from such a faith. And though many might not say so, it is a belief in God. A belief that justice rules in history, that the spirit of the eternal is watchful over the ways of man.

America inherited all that the Old World had to offer — both the good and the bad. And the chance to sift them out, the chance to separate them. The opportunity to build a nation that could be a beacon light to other nations — the nations of the oppressed and persecuted, longing to be free.

At times, our light has shone with a steady brightness — and the world has known new hope. At other times, it has grown dim — and hope has died. There is not much time left now to bring it back to brightness: but if we fail, the whole world will be dark.

20. Conclusion

And now — what hope is there that the American people will understand and act? The hour is late. The days of opportunity have nearly passed. What once we might have done almost with ease, we can now do only with great and increasing difficulty. No longer can the people of the United States win peace for themselves and security for the world on the terms that were available twenty, or ten — or even five — years ago. Choices once broad have narrowed. Whether they will broaden again will be decided by what is done with the choices that are left.

Some of these choices are military, others political and diplomatic; but the most important — indeed, all of them at last — are moral. Will we do right — that is the question — between ourselves and among all nations? If it is guidance that we need, we have it not only in the Scriptures of the great religions but in our own history and from our own exemplars. Loving one's neighbor as oneself and the equal rights of all are two expressions of the same principle. Doing unto others as we would that they should do unto us is the maxim that sums up the democratic way of life. " Ye cannot serve God and Mammon " is the declaration of the supremacy of the moral over the material, human welfare over money, the service of humanity over gain for oneself.

" Let us believe that right makes might," said Lincoln.

Which does not mean in the least that we can do without military preparations. Or that a resolution passed in a conference is the equivalent of a battalion. Right is not a substitute for might. Right makes might in the sense that to have a clear conscience liberates the best that is in us and resolve is fortified and strength of purpose increased. It also means that the universe is ruled by law, and that no matter how much evil may seem to triumph, justice wins the final victory. If our cause is just, if we are worthy of it, if we serve it wholeheartedly, the laws of God are with us.

We have not sufficiently remembered this. It is not that we have done badly in all respects. In some, we have done well. We have fed the hungry, succored the needy, defended the oppressed, resisted the aggressor, pled for peace. But we have also distrusted — many of us — our great traditions and we have lost confidence in our freedoms. We have let loose fear and misgiving among us. Instead of girding ourselves with unity in a righteous cause, we have sown suspicion and dissension; and in frustration and bitterness we have turned to persecution. All this the world has seen, and nothing we can now do will erase it from the pages of history.

Moreover, such behavior carries consequences. The years have passed and they were years of opportunity. They will not return. We must face the truth with courage: it is not morning now in America, with the sun just risen and a long day before us; the hour is late and if anything is to be done it must be done quickly, before the night descends upon us.

The fact is that even at best — even if we do well — our task is immense: greater perhaps than any nation has ever undertaken before us. Civilization — and perhaps man-

kind itself — will be blotted out within the present generation unless we find the wisdom to prevent it. We need
calmness of judgment and deliberation. We need steadi-
ness. We need the unity which at present we so woefully
lack. We need patience and endurance. We need faith
in God and in ourselves and one another. We need tireless
courage. We need all the resources of our minds and
hearts, and our need is greater than ever before in history.

Communism is the enemy. But we cannot defeat it by
remaining as we are. We cannot shorten the struggle.
We cannot subdue it by force of arms without inviting —
even if we won — a measureless catastrophe. We must
wear it down. We must resist its aggressions and be alert
to its conspiracies. We must out-plan it, out-perform it.
We must carry our way of life to a level that leaves Communism a hopeless and irrelevant contender. Our truth
must defeat its falsehoods, our liberty its servitude, our justice its oppressions, our compassion its cruelties, our faith
its cynicism, our humanity its degradations and debase-
ment.

We cannot do this if we lower our own standards and
betray our principles. That is why we must rebuke those
who say that they are fighting Communism but who are
careless of our moral values. They could all too easily lose
us the battle. For the struggle is not between Communism
and a debased democracy: that would be a struggle that we
could not win. The real struggle — and the one we can
win, and must if we are to survive — is between Communism and democracy's moral values.

It will not, however, be enough merely to maintain
these values in our way of life: we must *advance* them.
This has always been the American purpose. The Pilgrims

who gave us our northern tradition and the Virginians who charted our liberties were all alike in this: they wanted not alone a land of wider opportunity but a country where life could be more nobly lived. And because they had the vision of it for themselves, they had it for the world.

To win the present struggle requires not only the defense of elementary virtues, such as truth-telling, abstaining from bearing false witness, fair play in distinguishing the guilty from the innocent — these are, or should be, obvious restraints — but also an increased benevolence, a more sensitive concern for human welfare, a commitment to righteousness that can give the world a basis for security, a foundation for a happier future, and undergirding for peace.

What perils the immediate future holds for us we do not know. Our enemy down to now has been relentless. We are bound to hope that he will change. All other tyrannies, when their time had come, were overthrown. His, too, will not remain forever. If we can find the wisdom to avoid a suicidal conflict, we can defeat him with our faith, our purpose, and our way of life. But to do this, we must carry the benefits of our way of life — with all its rights and liberties — to all within our orbit. And certainly, we cannot do it by betraying at home what we wish to carry abroad. The dynamics of Communism must be met and outmatched by the moral force of a resurgent and regenerate democracy from which all bitter things are washed away.

Can we do it? The answer is the same that it has always been. The power of it is in us. God breathed it there from the beginning. But only we ourselves can call it forth.

Index